The Road from Ballymac

MICHAEL RYAN

WITH TOMÁS McCARTHY

www.**HERO**BOOKS.digital

HEROBOOKS

PUBLISHED BY HERO BOOKS
1 WOODVILLE GREEN
LUCAN
CO. DUBLIN
IRELAND

Hero Books is an imprint of Umbrella Publishing
First Published 2020
Copyright © Michael Ryan and Tomás McCarthy 2020
All rights reserved

ISBN 9781910827239

Cover design and formatting: jessica@viitaladesign.com
Ebook formatting: www.ebooklaunch.com
Photographs: Inpho and the Ryan family collection

Dedication

To my mother Maureen,
And Catherine, Michelle, Louise, Sinéad and Shane.
To my extended family, and all the players and mentors
with whom I enjoyed some great days
down through the years

Contents

Acknowledgements

ON FRIDAY OCTOBER 18, 2019, I got a text from Liam Hayes informing me that Hero Books were launching a series of books, and asking me if he could send me a proposal. I didn't reply but he sent me a second text three days later.

I rang him and we arranged to meet in the Horse and Jockey Hotel three weeks later. Liam is quite a persuasive fella and after a chat I somewhat reluctantly agreed to give it a go.

The principal reason for writing this book is to highlight the wonderful ladies football players from Ballymacarbry and Waterford with whom I shared some fantastic days. Very often women don't get the credit for the quality of the football they produce.

I inherited my love of sport from my late mother Maureen, an incredible woman who followed and supported us through good and bad days all over the country. To her and my father Tom, my brothers Willie and Pat, and my sisters Marian, Chrissie and Bernie, thank you for the great times we had growing up.

Plenty of fun and lots or great memories.

Thanks to Catherine and our four children, Michelle, Louise, Sinéad and Shane for the continuous support that has enabled me to devote so much time to my hobby and also for giving me so much enjoyment watching them play. Those games are etched in my memory.

Thanks to The Nire and Fourmilewater GAA clubs with whom I played – to play with your friends is special and we had some success along the way.

Thanks to Séan and Dolores Guiry. Séan and I have been partners in a building firm for 41 years, and thanks also to the lads who have worked with us, some great characters who ensured that there was never a dull moment. Ger McGrath springs to mind, his advice was usually worth listening to.

Thanks to all the people who offered me support and encouragement which I really appreciate.

And to Tomás McCarthy, thank you especially for being so thorough and professional as you worked with me on this book. We had many laughs and cups of tea in The Park Hotel. Tomás is blessed with patience and a sense of humour, two ingredients that made this project a great experience.

Thirty-two years ago I wrote the Fourmilewater Hurling Club history, so I have an idea of the time and effort that Tomás had to put in to this body of work.

Finally, I hope you enjoy reading this book, and that for many of you it brings back memories that we shared and enjoyed.

Michael Ryan
October 2020

◄ ◄ ◆ ► ►

THE OPPORTUNITY TO work with two All-Ireland winners on my first book was too good to turn down.

When Liam Hayes contacted me about this project last November, it was an immediate yes.

Writing a book is a much bigger beast than writing an article and Liam guided me through that process. He was always at the end of the phone to offer advice and encouragement. Still...

What have we got ourselves in for?

That's what me and Michael thought when we sat down for the first time.

I shouldn't have worried. Michael was a pleasure to deal with from start to finish. He threw himself head first into this project. He doesn't do things any other way.

We spent many Monday evenings in The Park Hotel in Dungarvan with tea and biscuits. We always got the special biscuits! Michael always wanted the best!

Two or three hours flew by in his company. He recalled each story, each game, each moment as if it happened yesterday. I could just sit back in my chair!

It was hard work but it was enjoyable.

I pushed Michael and he pushed me. No subject was off limits.

Michael always answered the question even if he didn't always like it!

During one of our phone calls during the lockdown, Michael told me, 'I want this to work out for you'.

That's him in a nutshell. I'll never forget those words.

Growing up in Ballymacarbry, I was aware of ladies football and Michael Ryan from an early age. Ballymac is the *home* of ladies football. There should be a sign in the village.

The Monday after an All-Ireland win, the team visited the National School and the cup was brought around to each class with sweets inside. 'Homework off,' was met with the biggest cheer!

When Michael was appointed Waterford hurling manager in 2011, I was starting out with the *Waterford News & Star* and reported on his highs and lows.

Despite the local link, I didn't treat him any differently and he didn't treat me any differently. I had a job to do and he had a job to do. It's important to be fair and balanced. I took the same approach to this book.

Thanks to Ger Lawton for giving me a break 10 years ago in the *News & Star*. I couldn't ask for a better sports editor.

To the one and only Phil Fanning for recommending me to Liam, and the rest of my colleagues in the press box for your help over the years.

To Michael Byrne and Liz Reddy in WLR for opening so many doors, like commentating on big matches and presenting a weekly GAA show. I really wish that my late sports editor Kevin Casey was around to read this.

To Deirdre O'Shaughnessy, during my college days in UL, for believing in me as sports editor of *An Focal*. That got the ball rolling.

To my wonderful parents whom I love so much.

My Dad Pat brought me to my first GAA match in 1998. I always brought a pen to mark the scores in the programme! We went to Croke Park three times that summer, including the ladies replay between Waterford and Monaghan. I was hooked after that.

My Mam Margaret gave me my interest in reading and writing, and for that

I will be forever grateful. The proof-reading at the start was much appreciated as well!

To my sisters Áine, Róisín and Ailís for your support. I'm so proud of you.

To my amazing girlfriend Brenda for backing me through thick and thin, putting up with me during the Covid lockdown and also doing some proof-reading along the way!

To Michael's family, Catherine, Michelle, Louise, Sinéad and Shane for giving this book your blessing.

I hope I have captured the man.

Tomás McCarthy
October 2020

PROLOGUE

Prologue

August 7, 2013

I DIDN'T HAVE any indication that there was a problem until Pat Grant rang me.

I got the phone call on Wednesday night, just after 10.30pm. Pat told me that the Waterford players wanted a change of management.

'Oh?'

I was very surprised.

For once in recent times we'd given Kilkenny a proper game of it. We lost 1-22 to 2-16 after extra time. I remember Brian Cody telling me after that he thought they were gone. Above all the games I was ever involved in, the feedback from the supporters was incredible.

A lot of people loved the style of hurling we played that night.

Derek McGrath texted me.

He was sitting beside one of my daughters at the game, and he told me that he doubted if he'd ever seen any Waterford team play with such pride and such passion.

I felt it was the start of something.

My term was up.

My two years were done. I was asked after that game if I wanted another term? 'Absolutely... no question about it. It's up to the county board.

'My name will be in the hat... as I imagine will the rest of the management team.'

Jimmy Payne told me that he felt that there were one or two people possibly working behind the scenes. He was saying that before the year was over.

What that was based on?

I don't know.

Myself and Pat Flanagan had started to plan for the coming year. We had one or two meetings down in The Ramada Hotel. Maybe I was foolish to assume that we would be reappointed.

I was very surprised.

Then again, looking back, nothing should surprise you. I'd seen enough over the years to know that these things do happen.

I couldn't believe it.

I honestly couldn't believe it.

The players were having a meeting on the Sunday morning. And I knew it was going ahead.

August 8

The following morning, at 9am in Lawlors Hotel in Dungarvan I met the county board and they filled me in on it.

'If I were you, I'd stay put,' one of the officials advised me. 'The county board will certainly elect you again. What I would do… I would get all the players into a room and open the door… and say if anyone wants to walk out… they can walk out now.'

'What happens if everybody walks out?' I replied.

I'd seen what happened with Justin McCarthy in Limerick.

'No,' I said, 'I'm not going down that road.'

August 9

It was very much up in the air.

I spoke to Kevin Moran. He was away. His said his head was fried from the whole thing. I spoke to Brick as well. The bottom line was I knew that they were going to have the meeting. I decided that whatever was going to happen, let it happen.

I didn't go ringing a dozen players trying to change their minds.

August 10

I was at Clonmel Óg GAA club on Saturday evening.

They had a function, and I was invited as manager of the Waterford senior hurling team.

I still knew the players' meeting was going ahead, there's no point saying otherwise. I knew what was coming down the tracks.

I did. I had a fair idea what was on those tracks.

August 11

I remember exactly where I was.

I was in the Millfield watching The Nire playing football against Ballylanders. Noel Connors rang me. He jumped right in. 'We had a meeting… and the players decided they want a change.'

'Fair enough!'

What else could I say? And that was it.

It was very courteous.

Noel is a nice fella.

I rang Timmy O'Keeffe, the secretary and told him I was pulling out. At the end of the day, if the players aren't happy they can just stop playing.

That was it. Decision made.

At the same time, I was just so disappointed. And, the next thing, the phone starts ringing. Right, left and centre.

People giving out, people complaining.

Waterford were playing Kilkenny in the All-Ireland minor semi-final that day. I spent a good bit of that game on the phone, talking to Pat Flanagan and one or two other people. Speaking to Pat was the defining thing for me. His advice was solid. He said he wouldn't advise me to throw my name in the hat because, if the players don't want somebody, they can decide to stop playing and then all the support will soon dwindle. The proof of that was in Limerick with Justin.

That night, I went to my local pub, Doocey's and I had a couple of pints! When I walked in, there was total silence.

It was like John Wayne had walked through the doors in a western movie, not me!

Everybody looked around, and everybody went silent. After about 60 seconds,

I moved down to my little corner.

I'd always go in on a Sunday night. A championship game, a league game, a win or a loss, it didn't matter. I'd go in at twenty to eleven, for an eleven o'clock closing. Doocey's is a pub you wouldn't be staying all night once Tony calls time!

We had our own little corner.

People like Pat Power, Thomas Kelly, Jim Wall and Brian Norris; we'd sit down and have a chat. It's interesting to hear what people think. I believe you need to be able to do that. That's unwinding.

I wasn't going to go hiding. I went on as if nothing had happened, and as if I had nothing to hide.

I *had* nothing to hide.

No point in crying about it.

Someone broke the ice.

My resignation had just been announced on *The Sunday Game*.

I remember that distinctly.

◄ ◄ ◆ ► ►

THE NIGHT BEFORE the 1979 county intermediate final I suggested that we all go to the pub!

I was trainer, selector and player with Fourmilewater that year. We had a meeting down in the hall and I noticed the players were very nervous. I decided that any fella who wanted to have a drink or two should have it. But no more than two.

The owner, Tony Doocey was a selector at the time and he had left the meeting before I had told the players. We went into Doocey's and a couple of lads started ordering pints.

Tony's eyes nearly jumped out of his head!

What's going on here?

I could see him having that conversation with himself.

'I told them to have a pint or two,' I explained. 'It won't do them any harm.'

There was no need to mind fellas. Some fellas came to the pub and had a mineral. I knew damn well that if that didn't work, I'd be in trouble the following day.

We were playing our neighbours, St Mary's from Touraneena. The build-up was unreal. Take Ballinamult Creamery, where supporters from both teams would meet. There were stories of a lot of bets being put on.

Bob Keane drove down through the village in his little van with the Touraneena colours on show. Nobody wanted to lose. The supporters didn't want to lose just as much as the players. It was a local derby, the first time ever in a county final. An awful lot at stake.

A lot of lads had played together at underage on the Fourmilewater minor hurling and The Nire under-21 football teams. They beat us in the Western final and beat us convincingly. They were miles ahead of us. There was a lot of doom and gloom around the place, a lot of soul searching.

IT WAS A miserable morning; the weather was bad. But it cleared up around match time. We just took off. We got three early goals. Jim Wall got two and Paddy Joe Ryan got one.

The day cleared up then, and we had seven or eight points of a lead and kept that cushion all through. A county title for Fourmilewater was a big deal because we hadn't won one in so long

We reversed what happened in the Western final.

Jim Wall described it as the most important win he ever had, and he had played in some big games. Mick Connolly was 39 years of age and played corner-back. He had dropped himself for the Western semi-final. He trained really hard for the next five or six weeks for the county final.

To see Connolly going out and leading from the front and putting in the tackles early on, it was a fantastic feeling. It was as good a win as I ever had on the pitch.

But I never used that approach again!

It was a typical 'Quit while you're ahead' scenario!

◄◄◆►►

August 12

On the Monday night, I was sitting down at home and the land line phone rang. I had been sitting in the same chair at home a few days earlier when Pat Grant called me.

'Michael Ryan... Jimmy Barry-Murphy here!

'I just want to say I can't believe what happened. The same thing nearly happened me.' The man had gone to the trouble of looking up my number.

Ger Loughnane sent me a nice text and told me I did a good job. 'The problem now is they're all looking for Mr Magic and there's no Mr Magic.'

The phone was hopping from the minute the news broke. Loads of people texting and ringing. The same words... 'I can't believe what happened.'

EVER SINCE THAT day, there's not one week that goes by that people don't tell me how disappointed they were. I'm still meeting people giving out about that decision. Not alone from Waterford, from all over the country.

I'd say for the first month, I must have met 500 people.

For a week, that support helped. It did. But six months later, when somebody says it, it isn't that you're annoyed by it, it's just that you've moved on from it and suddenly it's fresh in your mind again.

I know people who haven't gone to games since. I know serious Waterford supporters who have not gone to a game since. I'd like to tell them... 'Look, it's gone... it's done. I've long moved on'.

It's like everything in life. If you're sick and you don't die quickly, people lose interest. Within a couple of days, it's always about something else.

It happened with a couple of Waterford managers. What happened to me was just another chapter.

◄◄◆►►

I WAS IN The Berkeley Court Hotel in Dublin, when Ger Loughnane was named Philips Sports Manager of the Year in 1995.

I got the October award. Waterford had won their fourth All-Ireland senior title in five years. I would have regarded it as a big step up for ladies football, to be in that elite company.

I ended up in the early evening with the former Dublin manager, Tommy Lyons and Michael Lyster, and we had a good few pints! We stayed until late in the evening!

It was a coup for ladies football rather than a personal award for me. I always felt that managerial awards were a reflection of how the team was doing.

We were at our peak in 1995. We had 92 sessions that year… 75 training sessions and 17 matches. Everybody was at training early. We stepped it up to five nights a week. Five nights a week in 1995.

There were times we trained Friday, Saturday and Sunday. While we were doing that, the Dublin-based girls were training away on their own with Biddy Butler.

I walked around the back of the Hogan Stand before the All-Ireland final and this Monaghan fella shoved a flag in my face.

'Ye're going down today!'

I told the girls in the dressing-room. Jesus, they couldn't wait to get out. One of our underage selectors Ger Mooney was in the tunnel and they came out, and one of them hit him a belt of a shoulder and pushed him up against the wall.

They were driven that day. They were on fire.

We won the toss and it was over at half-time. We were unbeatable that day. We'd have beaten most teams that had ever played.

4-14 to 1-5.

Eighteen points. The biggest ever winning margin in a final. That was the day it all came together.

I was sad leaving Croke Park. I knew we'd never hit that peak again. That was the day when every single player was at nine and a half out of 10; I don't do 10 out of 10! I couldn't see us reaching that level again, and we didn't reach that level again. That's the trouble with this whole thing.

It consumes you.

I'D BE ON the bus leaving Croke Park, and I'd start thinking about next year.

That's what it did to me anyway. You couldn't really celebrate it because you're thinking about next year again. I always enjoyed it but I couldn't stop thinking ahead.

It changed after winning the second All-Ireland in 1992.

Ballymacarbry had won five All-Ireland club titles at that stage. It was all about the future. *Forget about that… let's move on.*

In the early years, it was absolute euphoria. It was like climbing Everest. But the more you won, the more you forgot about it straight away and instantly you started thinking about next year. It takes over your life to that extent.

The first couple were magical. As you get to win more championships, especially at club level, the minute the final whistle had gone, the minute the cup was being presented, the minute we were on the team bus, my focus used to turn to how many of these players will be around next year. *Are there any new players coming through? What else can we do to get better?*

I remember Séan Boylan saying one time that it takes over your life, and he was right.

◄◄◆►►

August 15

Championship Matters on RTÉ Two.

Marty Morrissey is looking at me.

Marty Morrissey: 'I get the feeling Michael Ryan, you want this job… would I be right to say that?'

Me: 'Of course I want this job. I think I have something to offer. I have maybe a different style of management to other people… I believe in assembling a good backroom team and delegating. Every facet of our backroom team was outstanding… and I think I have a lot to offer. Going forward I hope to be involved in Waterford hurling in the future.'

Marty Morrissey: 'So really, what you're saying is you are going to go for it?'

Me: 'We'll have a serious look at it Marty… and see what happens.'

I DID THE *Championship Matters* programme with Marty on the Thursday. The researcher, Aoife Sheehan from Limerick rang me and asked me to come on the programme.

Why not? I thought.

My daughter, Michelle drove me up.

I knew I'd nothing to be afraid of… *I'll just tell my side of the story.* I wanted to make sure that the truth would be told. Liam Rushe and Joe Canning were on the same night.

I told my story. When I was doing that interview, I was considering all the options. Then, when I really weighed it all up I thought to myself… *I don't want the hassle of this!*

Driving back home from Dublin that night, myself and Michelle had a chat about it. She'd be very analytical and have a cool light of day look at something. We went through it, and I told her what I had decided... 'I'm staying away from it'.

I had thought it all through.

If I came back in... if the county board appointed me?

Where would that leave me?

Lose one or two matches... all the questions.

I felt that I was leaving it in a very good position. I was packing it in almost from a position of strength, with regard to the world and the public.

I've never doubted, not once since driving down that night from Dublin, that it was the right decision.

Disappointment remained, of course it did.

We were in a good place at that time. We got to an All-Ireland final since, and could have won it, but have we set the world on fire?

Would I have done any better?

I don't know. I don't like the term unfinished business, but I would have liked one more year to see what we could have done. The following year, we were relegated and only won one championship match.

I can't guarantee what we would have done but I would have liked one more year because there were a few young players coming through. Austin Gleeson came through. Ger Cunningham, a coach from Limerick, was with me for a few sessions. I had spoken to Ger. I felt I had him lined up.

We would have been looking at some of the older players, telling them their time was up. We would have been thinking about some fellas. We had spoken about that, that we needed to change things up, but never really pinpointed who.

It lingered for a little while, it did. It put me thinking about the whole thing. *Is it worth it? Is it worth what you go through? Is it worth the time you put in... the time everybody else puts in?*

You'd question your sanity... *Is this worth it?*

You probably think for a little while it isn't, but time is a great healer; other things happen and life goes on. If you let it get you down, it will get you down.

You just move on.

There's a new challenge around every corner. There's always somebody looking for a manager or a coach. St Mary's in Clonmel rang me up, and off we went again. I didn't really envisage going back to inter-county though. I didn't think that was going to happen.

I HAVE NO ambition to manage Waterford again.

People have mentioned it to me and people have suggested it to me, but I never gave it a second thought. I've had two or three approaches from other counties.

My ambition from now on is a bit of coaching or motivational stuff. I had my go at it. I was an inter-county hurling manager for six years. People might say Westmeath was only Division 2, but it was just as important to me.

I've done my time at it. I'm happy with my lot as regards that.

It's a full-time job to be honest about it, especially when you put travel into it. Look, I've done my fair share of driving.

I've driven for the last 40 years.

◄◄◆►►

WHEN I'M DRIVING, I'm thinking. I jumped into the car one evening and drove over to Fitzgerald Stadium to see Kerry train.

Mick O'Dwyer would have been a big one for me.

I loved the brand of football Kerry played; that's why I went to see them train. I remember going down to Killarney in the summertime. The likes of Jack O'Shea would be out an hour before training, kicking the ball over the bar. Catch and kick.

They'd handle the ball 50 times, every man, before they started training. Training was savage. O'Dwyer did some amount of running with them. If I was on holidays in Kerry, I might go to see them two or three times that week.

I was a Kerry fan all my life anyway.

Now, I love watching The Dubs playing.

I saw how the Kerry players worked with the ball. Cyril Farrell, he was the same in Galway. Kilkenny were something else. They were flaking one another! I went down to see them three or four times. I got to know Brian Cody over the years and I'd have huge respect for him.

If anybody thinks it's easy to manage Kilkenny, they couldn't be more wrong. There's a lot of experts in Kilkenny, telling everyone else what should have been done and what wasn't done.

We were on holidays in Galway one time and I said to my wife, 'We must see the Galway hurlers training with Cyril Farrell'. And we did. Down to Athenry we went. I saw this fella roaring and shouting like a bull! Farrell did a lot of work with the ball too. He mentally toughened up Galway.

One night we went to Tuam to see the Galway footballers train.

It was 1983, before that infamous final against Dublin which ended with 12 men beating 14. We were sitting in the stand and Mattie McDonagh, the Galway manager, came over to me.

'Who are you?' he asked me.

I told him my name.

'What are you doing here?'

He thought I was with The Dubs! 'Listen', I said, 'where I come from there's no need to worry about us! I'm from Waterford… we're no threat to you!'

I've always gone to see teams training. Always good reasons. Can I get an edge? Can I learn something different?

Any advantage I tried to get it. If we were playing in Clare, I would think nothing of driving up to see the pitch before the match. I drove up to Miltown Malbay one time.

I drove up the Sunday before the match to see the pitch because we had never played there. That wouldn't cost me a thought. No surprises. I'd always step the pitch when I'd get there. Physically step the pitch.

Length and width. I know it's madness… but!

Like Fraher Field or Fitzgerald Stadium, you wouldn't need to, we played there a good few times. Two things about walking a pitch. Number one, you get a chance to think on your own. Number two, you get a good look at the pitch.

It was madness, but it was great!

YOU COULDN'T GO into any room in our house but you'd fall over a pair of football boots. Everybody in our house has played county and my wife, Catherine played for Ballymac and Waterford as well. Everything revolved around sport.

There was always a match. There was always a training session.

It was something we always did; it was something we always enjoyed. Looking back on it now, we got a great return from it. We had fantastic times all over the country.

LEGENDS SERIES

Michelle is the eldest. She is very similar to me. If she lost a game, she wouldn't talk. She'd go into a shell, and I'd be the same. I wouldn't be very chatty if we lost a game. I'd probably sit at home and have the video in my back pocket, and I'd be looking at it nearly before I got out of the car.

She has the same interest, the same passion and the same enthusiasm for it.

Louise played the game, enjoyed the game and loved the physical battle of the game. She was passionate about it but, once it was over, it was *over*. She wouldn't be like Michelle or even Sinéad. Shane is a bit like Michelle as well, he takes defeat poorly.

Sinéad had a Waterford jersey and a pair of shorts because she was a mascot from about three years of age. She'd tog out in the Waterford gear, come out to the front of the house with the ball; she had her own water bottle, and she'd solo run around the house.

I'd have the stopwatch timing her.

She'd sit down for a drink of water and off she'd go again.

When I was asked to go with Laois, Sinéad travelled up with me in the car. For about nine or 10 weeks in 2001. Sinéad was 10. If we were going to Laois at six o'clock, she'd be in the car at five o'clock!

Then Shane came along and he was more into the hurling, although he loved all sports including football and soccer.

The three girls were mascots for Waterford. Michelle was mascot in 1986. The three of them were mascots in 1993 and '94. Michelle then stepped away. In fairness, Louise would still be mascot, she's that kind of a character! It wouldn't bother her!

MY FATHER HAD absolutely no interest in sport. I'm not sure if he ever went to a match in his life; he probably didn't. Absolutely no interest.

My mother was a fanatic, never missed a game. She travelled the length and breadth of Ireland following teams and tore her hair out on a regular basis. If we were playing a match in Croke Park, she often disappeared behind the Hogan Stand before the match ended. She was a very intense person, she was very passionate.

They were polar opposites. I got my interest in sport from my mother and my mother's family. If you look at my father and his brothers and sisters, they all had

24

other interests.

In the 1998 All-Ireland final replay against Monaghan, there was still a few minutes left. My mother was at home watching the game on television, and she went out around the house and said a prayer. She couldn't stick it!

She went out the back door, walked around the house, came in the front door, into the kitchen and Siobhán O'Ryan had the cup in her hands when she came in. Siobhán was her niece!

My mother was the first person up at the Cross in Ballymac, or in Dungarvan, when the bus came back. She could be there two hours beforehand! She would pester someone to drive her!

The homecoming was huge. The biggest ever... 5,000 people. To go into the Square, where the Tour De France had passed a couple of months earlier, and see the place full!

That was the highlight, that was the pinnacle.

I'd love those days back again.

PART ONE

The Coaching Bug

« CHAPTER 1 »

THE MAN THAT changed my life, my GAA life, was Willie Prendergast.

Fourmilewater played under-16 hurling in 1970, and Tallow beat us 16-6 to 1-1. There were about 57 minutes gone and I thought we wouldn't score at all. We got a 21-yard free and Jim McGrath wanted to go for goal.

'For Jesus sake put it over the bar,' I remember telling him, '… or we won't score at all.'

THREE YEARS LATER, Willie Prendergast came into our club. He was originally a Christian Brother but he left the Brothers and became a lay teacher. He was teaching in a secondary school in Cashel and we got him down to train us.

Jesus he put us through hell.

A huge amount of running; push-ups, chin-ups, carrying one another on our backs and a fantastic amount of hurling.

Hooking.

Blocking and tackling.

Free-taking and lineballs.

Shooting practice and more shooting practice. He was ahead of his time. I couldn't imagine there were too many coaches doing hooking, blocking and tackling in those days. It made a big impression on me that you have to work on the skills. He absolutely transformed the team. We trained three or four nights a week.

He worked hard on us giving a savage commitment.

We were playing a game down in Ferryhouse, in Clonmel, against Carrick Swan one night. He was driving the car. There were a couple of fellas in the back of the car smoking. Willie stopped the car and put them out.

He took it that seriously.

Some of our players were from the neighbouring village of Touraneena. I think we had four of them. We trained there the night before the Western final and Willie gave everyone detailed A4 sheets of what we needed to do.

The really skilful fellas didn't have too many sheets, of course.

I had a good few sheets, though! I played midfield with Tommy Halpin. My twin brother Willie was in goal; he was the captain.

That August, we beat Tallow in the Western final by a point. After they beating us by 50 points, we turned it around. I'll never forget that day in Cappoquin. We went on to win the county minor title against Erin's Own. An A title!

It was played in Walsh Park before an All-Ireland intermediate final between London and Kilkenny. Waterford played New York in a National League game as well.

He gave us the winning mentality. He absolutely transformed a group of average players. In the first round of that championship, I was playing corner-forward, but he had me playing midfield by the end.

That experience lit a fire for me as regards coaching.

TWENTY-FIVE YEARS later, we had a get together for the team in Doocey's.

Willie was our guest speaker. He had a whole series of notes written out, he was so nervous. I was doing MC.

Just before we started, he ran up to me and said, 'I can't find the sheets! What am I going to do?'

'Willie!' I said, 'You know those lads… look down and everyone you see, say something about them. Your memory will do that for you.'

He did that and he got through it. Just when he was finished, he went back down and found he had the sheets pushed down between the seat!

I HAD NO interest in things that weren't done right.

In 1976, The Nire had a really good under-21 football team but we had no preparation done. We played Tallow in Cappoquin and we were beaten. I got a belt of an elbow and left three of my teeth out on the field. Walking off, I was giving out like hell.

'Jesus Christ… we had a team good enough to win the championship, if we had anyone to train us.'

A selector, who shall remain nameless, said, 'Why don't you do it?'

'I'll do it next year,' I replied.

I went to the AGM and it was up for grabs.

'I'll do it on one condition… that I'm the only selector,' I told everyone present. 'I'll do it myself… I don't want anyone near me.'

Then I was told that we were joined with Touraneena, so they had to have a selector.

'That's okay… we'll have one each,' I said.

Nobody was surprised that I put my name forward. The situation with the GAA in Ballymac, unfortunately, was that a lot of people were pushed into jobs at underage that they didn't want or didn't have any interest in doing. They were happy to see someone who was interested go and take it. In those days there was no queue of people who wanted jobs.

Our preparation in the years before that would have been very poor in football. We wouldn't have known any better. We went down to the Millfield and had one or two training sessions. We played a match, and most of the time we got beaten out the gate.

There were only one or two matches every year.

We didn't know what good coaching was until Willie Prendergast came along. We had seen what Tallow had done and in the back of our minds we were aware that there was something happening but we didn't know what it was. Willie Prendergast was a real eye-opener as regards coaching as far as I was concerned.

The players didn't have any problem with me taking over. All they wanted was someone to organise it because it hadn't been happening. We played a lot of challenge matches in South Tipperary and Waterford, and we did a fair bit of training.

John Dalton was the other under-21 selector, but he was playing with the county hurlers as well so he didn't have much time. We got to the Western final and John came into the dressing-room and he said, 'I wasn't involved all year… you work away!'

Believe it or not, we got no score in the second-half of the county final. We won it by six points to four against Dunhill/Butlerstown and no forward scored! There was a gale force wind blowing in Fraher Field. We were six points to two up at half-time and it was backs to the wall after that. Gerry Coffey got five of the six points, and Declan Fitzpatrick got the other one. Two midfielders!

We played with the wind in the first-half – something I've always tried to do. I believe that you always play with the wind, particularly if you're fairly fit. That fitness will stand to you in the second-half playing against the wind.

We won the county final and I met the same fella that said, 'Why don't you do it?'

'That's what should have happened last year,' I informed him.

I PLAYED UNDER-21 football for Waterford in 1976. No preparation.

A trial, meet two or three times and pick a team. I was an under-21 selector in 1978. Things were bad. We played Kilkenny in a challenge down in Waterford. I had to play myself; we only had 14 players!

I played corner-forward. I was two years overage!

I was on the senior panel for one year in 1984 and played a National League game up in Fermanagh. One game is all I played. We had a good session the night before! We went on the beer and that was it.

Previously, we were up in Longford and we went to see a rugby match. Ireland were playing rugby, and we were up there at one o'clock in the day; sure we just went to the pub, nobody said anything different.

At three o'clock in the morning, a selector said to me, 'What are you having?'

Imagine that?

Imagine that preparation!

Wouldn't that money have been far better spent on coaching and development?

Even though there were some good players, the whole thing wasn't taken seriously enough. I wouldn't have been good enough for it anyway. I was only an average club player, but it was an interesting experience!

IN FEBRUARY 1978, there was a hurling coaching course in Dungarvan and nobody in the club would go. I said I'd go.

Joe McGrath was giving it, with Ned Power of Tallow and John Hanley from

Clare. It was one of the first ever coaching courses in Waterford.

Ned Power made a very valid point that stuck with me always. 'You'll be down on the pitch with your players and you'll show them something a hundred times,' he said, '… and it won't go right and then some day, they'll perfect that skill.

'And they'll do what they're supposed to do brilliantly.

'You'll feel like you've won the sweepstake.' In Ireland at the time there was no lotto.

I was hooked. It was on over two weekends. That really convinced me about the potential of coaching and the merits of coaching properly.

The first thing was the attention to the skills of the game. The idea of training before that was backs and forwards, one or two laps and maybe three or four short sprints and that was it; you went home. I saw it in my own club.

This was about coaching the skills of the game; first touch, striking. That coaching course and what Willie Prendergast had done really convinced me that if you're going to win matches, you have to prepare properly. Somewhere before that the GAA had got lost in sub-standard training. Not enough emphasis on skill and touch.

Every training session after that, I used the ball 95 percent of the time.

Ned Power would have been an icon of coaching; well-known and well-respected around the county. He's from Dungarvan originally, then left to take up a teaching post in Tallow; played on the Waterford team that won the All-Ireland in 1959.

Tallow were struggling very badly until Ned Power came to town. He came and he transformed Tallow. We played against Ned Power at underage. Every time we played Tallow, I always felt that they were a well-coached, well-drilled team.

We suffered a couple of serious beatings from Tallow in underage over the years until we beat them in that minor final in 1973.

WE GOT CERTIFICATES and all that. I don't know where they are now! A coaching certificate was a big thing in those days.

I remember coming home from the course in the snow. It was on a Saturday. I went to see Tony Doocey's mother in hospital in Dungarvan. Coming out, the car got stuck in Colligan in the snow. Luckily enough I had a shovel in the boot and I was able to dig out the car. It took me four hours to get back to Ballymac.

A savage fall of snow.

People had to stay overnight. The cars were buried in the snow and there was the case of a bulldozer the following morning driving over a couple of cars. Thank God I got out of it. That's another thing I remember about that coaching course!

« CHAPTER 2 »

BALLYMAC BECAME SO accustomed to winning that the locals never asked us did we win? They asked us how much did we win by?

We were beaten in 1988; we weren't beaten again until 1996.

I met Tom Moore in Doocey's.

Tom is so quiet.

'And ye got beaten yesterday!' Tom said to me.

'We did,' I agreed.

'How did ye manage that?' Tom asked me.

That's how accustomed people had become to winning. And Tom would be a good friend of mine; I played hurling with him.

THE BALLYMACARBRY LADIES football club was founded in 1970.

Ardfinnan had a festival going for many years with men's football, and then women were added to it as another attraction. It was an absolute novelty, that's all it was.

It was a reason for people to come out and fundraise. There was a theory that it was such a novelty that the general public would turn out to see women playing football. Prior to that, it was unheard of.

Then a rivalry built up between Ardfinnan, Ballymac, Powerstown, and Newcastle. In that era, in Ireland, in the late 1960s and 70s, there were a lot of evenings and time to be filled in and nothing to do. That's basically how it started.

From Ballymac's point of view, it started off in the Paddock where the Pinewood factory car park is now. It was just a field behind the goals of the GAA pitch where the piggery was. They played a few games in the Millfield. Frankie Connolly was the trainer.

In those days, it was just girls looking for something to do. The Waterford County Board wasn't founded until 1971. It drew big crowds because, as I've said, it was purely a novel attraction.

The first championship was played. Ballymac won it, and it took off from there.

IN 1975, I was asked to train the team, and I just took it on for a year.

Coaching, as I've explained already, was in its infancy. It was just a question of working with the ball and working on the skills. It was very basic, there was no magic formula.

It wasn't very tactical in those days. Ladies football was a catch and kick game. There were no underage teams, so players didn't have any base. But they were interested.

There were no facilities to tog out. The girls had to change in their cars. No dressing-room, no showers, no frills. You had the wood and the trees around the pitch.

The river on the left.

It was always a pretty dry base.

There were a few humps and hollows thrown in. Then you had the midgets on a summer's evening. There's a large selection of midgets in the Millfield!

It was only 11-a-side. The affiliation fee for all the clubs was £2! Imagine that! We won the championship. We played Portlaw in Abbeyside. The final score was 2-6 to 1-6. Ann McCarthy scored a goal and five points.

I was there in 1975 and '76 but I had no great interest in it. I was playing myself. I was playing hurling and football. I wasn't the best player on the planet but I always believed in training and preparing. I would have been at every training session we had. I was also involved in a lot of underage coaching at that time.

There's only so many nights in a week.

I was a bit sceptical; I hadn't seen a lot of it. To be honest, I wasn't aware how good women could be when they prepared properly.

I don't have time for this, I thought.

IN 1982, MY wife, Catherine and my sister, Bernie persuaded me to train the team for a second time.

I think it was the June Bank Holiday; I was building a cattle grid out at the entrance to the front of the house. The two of them came out and they sat on the wall beside me talking away. Then, suddenly, Bernie brought it up. Catherine was only the back-up to Bernie!

They said to come down to the field… and I went down. I remember distinctly walking through the goalposts. The group was halfway down on the left hand side near the river doing a bit of training, and I was watching them.

It was very basic stuff they were doing; they were only playing a bit of a match. The first thing that struck my eye was this girl called Marie Crotty. She could do anything with the ball; she could make the ball talk.

I said I'd take a session.

I wouldn't say I was hassled into doing it, but it was bordering on hassled!

MY BIGGEST FAILING was that I was too hard on people related to me. I've dropped my sister, dropped my daughters and dropped my wife. If you were related to me, you were at a disadvantage.

People are either too easy or too hard on their own.

I was very hard on my own. I'd seen too much favouritism, even in my own area. I'd seen fathers picking sons. That was a bugbear of mine now.

I dropped my wife one time and there was no word spoken in the house for a week! I thought she played very poorly on the day and that was it. It was back in the mid-80s.

Overall, she has been a great support to me no doubt about that.

Bernie captained Waterford to win an All-Ireland in 1992 and the following year, she was taken off in an All-Ireland club semi-final.

She wasn't playing well on the day.

I remember taking off Michelle against Cork in 2004. The first day Cork beat us. I probably shouldn't have taken her off looking back on it. I came to the end of the road in 2006. I had three daughters, and there's no point in the manager having three daughters on the team.

It was always in my head. *Don't favour your own too much.* I'd seen loads of examples of it around the GAA.

It drove me the other way and I was wrong.

WE GOT STUCK into it. I put them through a savage session. Then, when I had it done, I said what I was planning next for them.

'Ye're so unfit,' I told them to begin with.

'We'll train again tomorrow night!'

I thought there'd be no one there.

There were two extra there. It went from 15 to 17.

A huge amount of running. Men's training which probably wasn't suitable for women. Push-ups, chin-ups and running, running… running with no ball.

Sprinting.

Long runs.

And everything else. It nearly killed them. They never did that before. By God they didn't shy away from it. One or two girls got sick. Physically sick.

No resistance though. The next night there were the 17 and we worked away.

We were ahead of our time as regards training. Ladies football teams, by and large, weren't training as hard as that. We had a couple of skilful players as well. In two weeks, you could see the improvement because they wanted to get better.

When you're coming from that level and you start preparing, you see a big improvement early on. The first 10 steps on the ladder are the easiest steps to take. The initial progress was easily made as regards fitness. When you're halfway up the ladder then it's more difficult to get to the top.

After a week, it was on to skills. Using the ball; a lot of emphasis on kicking, blocking down, hand passing, movement, one-twos.

We played a lot of seven-a-side football.

The ball was up and down the field very fast. We went from defending to attacking. An emphasis on everyone being able to defend and everyone being able to attack, and everyone being comfortable on the ball.

If you're comfortable on the ball, you can play.

We had tight panels so we'd only have 16 or maybe 18 players; everyone was involved instantly in the game. People like the chance to score. If you play backs and forwards, what's in it for the backs? It's very hard to motivate yourself.

If you put the backs against the forwards in a competitive instance, in a game, and the backs get a goal. 'Jesus lads what's gone wrong here? The backs are scoring goals… where are ye gone?'

Very soon, you build up the competitive thing.

Everybody loves to score and everybody loves to win. Always at the end of training, we played a game. And 20 push-ups for the losing team! Nobody wanted to be doing those push-ups! The winners counted them for the losers!

And almost goaded them when they were doing it. It was good fun but it became very competitive. You start at it, you see it develop; you get better and, suddenly, it's like a drug. It's in your system.

THE COUNTY FINAL against Dunhill was a tough battle, but they were an ageing team and we were a young team. We always felt that once we weren't blown away at the start, we had the youth and we had the fitness down the stretch.

Marie Crotty scored a goal from a penalty. They had some good players, like Nellie McGrath and Ann Murray. Serious footballers. At half-time, it was obvious they were gasping for breath and we had a younger team. We knew we had the fitness levels.

The big memory I have is sitting in Stradbally.

Eileen Fitzpatrick bought me a pint of Guinness.

I was sitting down and thinking… *This is the end of this.*

Then someone asked, 'When is the Munster Club Championship?' I nearly died! I had a black jumper on me and a blue hat. In those days, there was no fancy tracksuits going. You had a pair of football boots and a pair of football socks, and you were in civilian fashion after that.

I was sitting down having a drink and the Munster Club Championship was starting. *Jesus.* I couldn't believe it.

We trained twice a week right through the winter. I think we took one week off for Christmas. We played in the middle of March, inside in Clonmel against Slievenamon who had beaten Ballymac several times. We beat them and the players couldn't believe it because they had been hammered in Ballymac.

We beat them because we had a young team and we were training right through.

Then came that famous Munster final in Ballyclough. I just couldn't believe where it was played.

A farmer's field. Half a goalpost on one side. A soccer goal! The posts didn't extend beyond the crossbar.

On the other side there was one post up, and there was a bit of lime on the pitch. It was like a few buachalans had been pulled to play a game. Cow shit all over the pitch. The corner flag up on a buachalan.

I'll never forget it!

I couldn't believe it; still can't believe it.

We were playing a Cork team. They were a damn fine team, St Enda's. The score was 1-6 to 0-2. They beat us and we had to go again.

WE WERE VERY unhappy with the refereeing in the Munster final in 1984.

St Enda's again.

A Kerry referee.

Brigid Grant scored a goal and the goal was disallowed. When the game was over, I marched up to him.

We had a guy doing the video. It was a camera he got in from America and there was a monitor and all on it. It was ahead of its time like. We were able to see what happened.

'Why did you disallow the goal?' I asked the ref.

'She was inside the square!' he replied.

We showed it to him.

'She was not inside the square... she ran 10 yards!'

'She fouled the goalie,' he then told us. I tore into him verbally.

The following Wednesday, I got a letter. I was summoned to a Munster Council meeting in the Hibernian Hotel in Mallow. There was a pub quiz on in Doocey's the same night and I was taking part. The meeting was on at half past seven, so we reckoned we would be up and back for the quiz. Brigid Grant was with me; she had said something to the referee as well.

We walked in and who was chairing the meeting? The referee.

It didn't take long.

Six months suspension. For me.

Brigid got six months as well.

She stayed on at the meeting, and I went home. They couldn't get a secretary and they had to lift her suspension, so she could serve as secretary. The whole thing was a farce.

I got the six months but I didn't mind and you know why?

There were no matches on for six months anyway! I duly served my time!

WE FIRST STARTED videoing matches in 1982.

My wife was working in the glass factory and all the workers got the opportunity to buy a video recorder at a special rate. She gave me a present of the recorder. There was one tape with it. The 1982 World Cup.

I remember the first two lines on that tape. 'It began in Barcelona with a dove of peace… it ended in Madrid with triumph for Italy.'

I now had a video recorder. Then it was a question of finding somebody to do the videos. We had various people; there was an odd video camera here and there.

If we thought we were going to win the game by 30 points, we didn't video it. The county finals in 1982 and '83 were videoed. When we got into the Munster Championship, everything was videoed. I'd watch it back that night.

Very often, the entire team came into my sitting-room and watched the match. They weren't even big drinkers. They loved playing football. They'd get off the bus, might have one or two drinks; and come in and watch the match. A load of them sitting on the floor!

Imagine having 20 people inside in the sitting-room!

I would sit down the following night with my notebook. No one there only myself. Play maybe five minutes, pick up something, write it down, log it.

Wides and frees.

Silly frees given away… missed passes, bad handling errors.

Then we'd feed that information back into the players. Very often show the players what happened. There were a few late nights.

FAST FORWARD TO 1985 and the Munster Council had a problem getting a referee. I was at the meeting, and I said I would get a Tipperary referee. I got Tom Lonergan from Newcastle. Tom was from over the road but he was a very fair fella.

He didn't give anything we shouldn't have got.

Castleisland missed a penalty in the first-half. Marie Crotty went into goal for the penalty. We always did that in those days. She was a big-name player and we always felt it would put pressure on the penalty taker.

She had a very good record on penalties, stopped a lot of them.

Five points to one was the score in that game. We were a lot better than them. It was our fourth year at it. We had been beaten in 1982, '83 and '84. If we had lost again, I don't know would we have come back.

It was a tense kind of a game. If they got a goal, anything could have happened. It was a question of getting over the line. We just wanted to win the game and after that the whole thing took off. That was the confirmation that this team had arrived. It was a huge stepping stone for us to win a Munster final.

The Millfield was full for the All-Ireland semi-final against Hollymount from Mayo. The Dungarvan Pipe Band played and the teams paraded around the pitch. It was a massive occasion. Prior to that era, Ballymac would have played in county finals, won a couple and lost a couple. Ladies football was no big deal but suddenly here we were after winning a Munster final, going onto an All-Ireland semi-final and a crowd down from Mayo. Hollymount brought huge support, as Mayo always do.

There were a few stakes and ropes around the Millfield.

Ringed right around the pitch. There was a huge crowd at it and we won well the same day.

We lost to The Heath from Laois in the All-Ireland final. We were 1-4 to no score up at half-time after playing with a gale. We only scored two points in the second-half.

TWO YEARS LATER, we got back to the All-Ireland against Hollymount in Tullamore.

We had two 50-seater buses amongst all the cars. I remember Paddy O'Grady, a supporter, passed out the two buses coming into a turn.

I thought he was dead! I'll never forget that.

We had a following from day one. The parents bought into it straight away. Not alone parents, but aunts and uncles, sisters and everybody bought into it. We used to bring a 50-seater bus and there were only 20 players so we'd bring people on our bus.

My mother always used to travel on the bus.

In Tullamore, we were miles ahead of Hollymount. Marie Crotty was always outstanding. She was our best player. Bernie Ryan and Mari O'Ryan as well. We had a lot of young players on that team and they had ferocious hunger.

Marie Crotty and all those were in their early twenties. Áine Wall was only 17. The final itself was almost an anti-climax.

All that year we won our games easily. Fourteen points in the Munster final, 13 points in the All-Ireland semi-final, and 17 points in the All-Ireland final. We were very fit, very committed, everybody trained. Patricia Butler and Marie Crotty came back from Dublin every weekend for training. Everybody was around, nobody missed training and we won that championship easy enough.

« CHAPTER 3 »

TO SEE 56,000 people at Croke Park for an All-Ireland ladies football final was a great source of satisfaction to me.

I remember the 1983 final was played in Kilsheelan in Tipperary. No disrespect to Kilsheelan now. I was at it, Wexford played Kerry. I went down to that game to see what the standard was because I was after getting involved with Waterford. I remember sitting on a concrete stool in Kilsheelan on a lovely summer's day to see an *All-Ireland final*.

Waterford weren't fielding teams at the time so we decided to represent the county. It was an entire Ballymacarbry team.

We started at a very low ebb.

I remember we got to the Munster final in 1984 and we were well beaten by Kerry, 5-9 to 0-3. In 1983, '84 and '85, we struggled; got very badly beaten in 1985. Then, we decided to be regraded down to junior. We sent Brigid Grant and Noel Murray off to a Munster Council meeting and we got regraded. We didn't have to make much of a case.

We felt that we had to go back and build again. The hidings we were getting were no good to anybody. It was no good for team morale; we hadn't enough players and Kerry were very strong at the time. We were miles away from it.

I like slow progress because slow progress is going to last.

A quick fix doesn't ever last. All I ever asked for is a group of people who are interested. I'm not worried about what standard they are; senior, junior, intermediate… whatever they are. Once you get a group of people that are interested, want to succeed and work hard, that's what it's all about.

IN 1986, WE played a county final down in Kilmacthomas against Newtown and they nearly beat us, so we drafted three of them onto the county panel – Colette Whyte, June Whyte and Nora O'Sullivan. Two of them made the starting line-up after that. Now we had three players from outside the club and over the next 10 years we built on that.

There were only two senior clubs to pick from. We were strong, Newtown were strong and Stradbally had a bit of a team.

Once we came out of Munster, we knew we were okay. We won the All-Ireland semi-final up in Mayo. We played Wexford's second team in the final. It was the first game of ladies football ever played in Croke Park. It made people sit up and take notice.

◄ ◄ ◆ ► ►

CROKE PARK WAS the mecca. It was the place.

There was an aura about it, there was a magic about it. If you got in there, you're dealing with the best and playing against the best. Any player or manager or spectator should be saying… 'I can't get enough of this'.

In 1970, when I was only 15, Frankie Connolly asked me would I be interested in going to the All-Ireland. Séan McCarthy came with us; Johnny Coffey and myself. I somehow got permission from my mother to go. I was only 15 like. My father probably didn't know. We kind of kept it quiet.

Frankie Connolly had a white Anglia car.

CZI388 was the number plate.

We headed to Thurles for the train. This was on a Friday night. We got to Dublin around seven or eight o'clock and we were traipsing around the quays looking for a place to stay. We eventually got a B & B at Essex House.

The following day we did the tour of Dublin. I remember going to Kilmainham Jail with the lads. That night, at the National ballroom, I couldn't get in because I was 15 but they got me in somehow. Under someone's coat!

Johnny Coffey wasn't used to Dublin, God be good to him. The following day, I remember Johnny saying, 'Are we walking up to Croke Park?'

And he might meet an odd person and say, 'Excuse me… are we on the right road to Croke Park?' And there were thousands walking! In fairness, it was the father figure coming out in Johnny. He was such a gentleman.

THE ALL-IRELAND football final.

Meath and Kerry. Johnny bought a big Kerry flag. We were together. The two lads, Séan and Frankie, were on Hill 16. We got two tickets from the hurling club… Cusack Stand… Lower Deck… the 50-yard line, halfway down underneath.

Every time Kerry got a score, Johnny jumped up.

This Meath fella turned around and he went crazy! The flag was going up in the man's face. 'If you lift that flag again,' he said to Johnny, 'I'll drive it down your throat!'

Johnny was completely silent. At some stage in the second-half, a fella called DJ Crowley got a ball about 70 yards out and he tore through the Meath defence, and unleashed a rocket to the top corner of the net.

Johnny yanked up the flag and drove it into your man's back!

He turned and it took two fellas to hold him back! How we weren't killed I don't know! Johnny had to move into the aisle and couldn't watch the rest of match!

We came back to Heuston, and the train was gone. We were very low on money; I think Frankie had a few quid anyway and put us up that night. We rang someone to tell my mother that I wouldn't be back.

We eventually got home to Thurles at three o'clock on Monday. We came into the village and I couldn't figure out why all the cars were there. A funeral was on. Someone had died and was almost buried while we were gone.

I went to loads of All-Irelands after that, but I'll never forget my first one. You see it on television; next thing you're there, a young fella from the country. I didn't expect to be back there as a manager.

◄◄◆►►

LADIES FOOTBALL HAD been trying to get into top venues for a few years.

The All-Ireland final was played in Páirc Uí Chaoimh in 1985. Noel Murray

‹‹‹ **MICHAEL RYAN** CHAPTER 3 ›››

from Waterford refereed it. That was a step-up.

So, the next logical step was to get into Croke Park. Pat Quill was President at the time and manager of the Wexford senior and junior teams. He had two teams beaten in All-Ireland finals and he had to go up and present the cups to Kerry and Waterford. He was the man who got ladies football into Croke Park.

From sitting on that stool in Kilsheelan to see it going to Páirc Uí Chaoimh, and then into Croke Park. They were huge steps.

Waterford hadn't played in an All-Ireland final in Croke Park since 1963. Twenty-three years. It was a big deal that way.

It was also a big deal for the players. They were really proud to represent their county. There was an eerie sound in the stadium. There was only a small crowd in the middle of the Hogan Stand. But we didn't care if there was nobody there. We were out in Croke Park and wanted to win the All-Ireland.

We won 4-13 to 0-0.

We expected to win it but we didn't expect to have it as easy as that. We were on a roll and got a couple of early scores. Marie Crotty got the first point in Croke Park, Caitriona Casey got a goal. We got a couple of early goals. We were just too strong for them.

Five minutes from time, I was in on the pitch and I remember saying to our full-back, Margaret Phelan… 'Don't worry about giving away a free'.

I didn't want to beat anybody scoreless.

We gave away a free anyway, and they missed it!

Someone said, 'They're not getting another chance!'

I mean it was very harsh on the Wexford team. Our girls were winners, like. Even in training, they were hopping off one another.

Margaret went up and collected the cup.

We relished Croke Park. Earlier on that year, 12 of those players lost an All-Ireland club final. We won a National League final; we beat Laois. We'd lost a couple of Munster club finals, we'd lost an All-Ireland club final, and they were just desperate to succeed. It was their time.

We came back to Lawlors Hotel in Dungarvan to a reception. The mayor was there and a few people. Family were around. There was a nice gathering but it wasn't in the Square or anything. It was in Lawlors Hotel.

Probably 200 people. No more than that definitely.

47

But they were 200 enthusiastic people and sometimes enthusiastic people can make an awful lot of noise! The girls brought the cup to Ballymac school, Kilrossanty school and Newtown school.

A Waterford GAA team hadn't won an All-Ireland since 1959. A Waterford GAA team hadn't played in Croke Park since 1963 in a championship match. That was almost a quarter of a century. It also caught a bit of imagination because it was the first ladies final played in Croke Park.

WE DEVELOPED A bit of a following. We were beaten in an All-Ireland club final earlier that year and we brought a big crowd to Leahy Park in Cashel so people were starting to follow the game.

Five hundred people were there for the homecoming in Ballymac on the Monday night. It was practically an entire parish turning out. Paddy Phelan always had a fire lighting. There was a big bonfire in the car park.

It was something that hadn't happened before. It was unique, it was new. People had latched onto it. People recognised that the girls were genuine about sport, trained hard and loved playing for Waterford.

In 1986, things were a lot different than they are today. You had to fight for recognition and fight for your rights. We didn't get a lot of coverage in the media.

I wrote all the match reports for the *Dungarvan Leader* and *Dungarvan Observer*.

I was often writing on my knee coming home on the bus. Until the day I gave it up in 2006. In later years, Michelle on Sunday nights typed up the reports that I had written and we faxed them into the papers.

The media scrum didn't kick in for ladies football until the All-Ireland final weekend, for about two or three days. It got great media attention then.

It was something that annoyed me over the years.

Everybody wanted a piece of the teams for the All-Ireland final but where were all those journalists in the weeks and months before it, and the weeks and months after it when there was a lot of good football being played?

It disappointed me.

I knew, and everybody else knew, that there were a lot of good footballers around the country and a lot of good games being played but the whole world was oblivious to how good the product was.

The sports highlights started coming on the television, then *The Sunday Game* in 1998 and then TG4 took over and what a job they have done since.

The best thing that happened to ladies football was TG4.

They made the whole world aware of the really good product that ladies football was. They brought it into people's homes right around the country. They started off doing the All-Ireland finals, then they moved back to the semi-finals, further back to the All-Ireland series; then they went to the club, then they went to the O'Connor Cup.

« CHAPTER 4 »

IF YOU WANT something done, ask a busy person.

When I took over the Waterford ladies, I realised that something had to be done so I became chairman of the county board in 1988 as well. I felt that the county manager had to be involved in organising club fixtures and everything else. It was easier. I was chairman for 15 years.

The whole thing had to be organised better. First of all, we had to find more clubs. We established something like 15 clubs in three or four years. We went from having three clubs to 17 or 18.

I had a good committee with me, people like Noel Murray, Eleanor Hickey, George Young and Ann O'Neill. We organised the whole lot and developed the clubs in the county.

We ran a good county board. When I stepped down as county board chairman in 2006, myself and Eleanor handed over €70,000 to the incoming executive. We had sponsorship from different bodies.

Waterford Foods were our first sponsors from 1986 to '91, then Bridge Terries in 1992, then Lawlors Hotel and then Saltan Properties with Michael Ryan. Michael gave us a serious amount of money in 1999, 2000 and 2001. Three years, money up front. The Dublin Supporters Club were brilliant to us, Ann Ryan in particular. Every year they gave us a cheque.

We had flag days and calendars as fundraisers. We sold flags in the pubs of

Dungarvan one night coming up to an All-Ireland final. We covered every pub in Dungarvan. Jesus, we made serious money. We had to do those things ourselves. It was an idea that George Young came up with. George was a fantastic organiser, as was Eleanor.

We had to generate the money. The money was to make sure that we could do our best for the players. We always got a great response. A lot of people, even though they weren't going to games, had pride in Waterford and they saw the girls were doing well and they had no problem in putting their hands in their pockets and throwing in a few quid.

I remember Austin Flynn gave me a 50 pound note to buy a couple of footballs for the girls. Austin was the Waterford full-back in 1959. People were doing that kind of thing. There was a lot of goodwill out there.

Noel Murray played a big part in the fundraising as well. He organised a calendar every year. He got 50 or 60 ads and people paid decent money to get their names in the Waterford ladies football calendar. Noel looked after that

Eleanor Hickey was a brilliant secretary from Touraneena who did everything. She organised buses, booked meals… you name it. Just ring Eleanor.

Bus on the moon at 9 o'clock?

She'd be there at 10 to nine. Absolutely brilliant. She made life a lot easier for me because I could concentrate on the team. It was one person doing the whole lot in the early days. Managing, training, coaching, all the physical work, sending off the team to the programme, all that stuff. Eleanor came in and she was massive. If I told Eleanor the team, nobody else would know it. I could really trust her.

In the early days, players paid to go on the bus and paid for their own food.

I paid.

Everybody paid.

Hallahan's bus from Cappoquin. That was until Noel Murray put a structure in place and George Young came along and did fundraising. We had it sorted by 1990.

THEN I GOT into underage.

That meant I was managing the Waterford under-16, minor and senior teams, and Ballymac, and I was chairman of the county board as well.

The under-16s were beaten by Dublin in the All-Ireland final down in Carlow in 1989. We kept at it. We won the four All-Irelands in 1991 (under-16, minor, senior and club). Ger Mooney was with those underage teams as well, a good lad. I also gave three years as Munster president, and managed Munster for several years.

When I started off as senior manager, I had no other selectors. Not for years. I was on my own until about the mid-90s.

That suited me down to the ground. You can take all the blame when something is going wrong. I'd seen it too many times in the GAA, with my own club and other clubs as well, that people took jobs and they just didn't do the jobs. You wouldn't see them. If you expect the players to train, then the mentors should be at training. I don't know any other system that works.

I'd generally pick the teams myself. I'd always consult with Brigid Grant but I had the final say. It worked for me at underage with my own club and maybe I got carried away with that.

You go to an AGM and what happens?

'You'll do it… you'll do it… you'll do it!'

That's what you hear, but most of the people with their arms pinned behind their backs don't 'do' very much after that AGM.

I was in control of it and I knew who was training. From day one, I always kept a record of training. There's still diaries at home.

Date… who trained… and who didn't train.

A zero for not being there… a one for being there… and a plus sign for being there but not training.

So, if anybody said anything to me, I could say, 'There's your record there in front of you'.'

BRIGID GRANT PLAYED a big part in our success at club and county as a number two. She was a very shrewd football woman and a tough character; she didn't give anything soft.

She also had the advantage of dealing with women.

You definitely need a woman with you. We always had a rule from day one; you can't be in the dressing-room when girls are changing. Brigid was always in and out, and she'd come and say, 'Everybody is changed now'.

Or she'd give out the jerseys. She did all those things.

Brigid was close to the players. Someone might be sick or someone mightn't be at their best or whatever. She was a sounding board.

She didn't spare anyone. It was no good a player whinging to Brigid that there was something wrong. She wouldn't give away anything soft, she would point it out straight away. Very good to weigh up the opposition. Very sharp.

She would have played with some of those players; she was the goalkeeper in 1986, and would have socialised with them and she would have known their mindset. If someone was out late or anything, Brigid would know it!

Now, we had very little of that, but Brigid would know those things. That was important.

Brigid had the ability to be firm on one hand, and also be a shoulder to cry on. She often spoke to players on her own. She was very good at doing one-to-ones with the players. She pulled away a player and had a word with her. She did so much work behind the scenes.

She wouldn't dish out praise for the sake of it. She had no favourites.

She'd tell someone straight up, 'You're not playing well'.

She certainly didn't mollycoddle anybody. If something needed to be called, Brigid wouldn't be afraid to call it.

The only little thing about her was that very often she got into trouble with referees! Brigid wouldn't be afraid to let the referee know what she thought. If she had a downside, that was it!

WE WERE COMPETITIVE in senior from day one.

People say it wasn't as competitive back then, but Waterford versus Kerry was fairly competitive I can promise you. We lost four Munster finals and four league finals. Eight major games in four years.

Jesus, eight defeats.

Kerry had some of the greatest players that ever played the game. Mary Jo Curran in the middle of the field, what a footballer! They had really good forwards like Eileen Lawlor and Margaret Flaherty. They had Mary Lane at centre-back. She kicked 45s over the bar for fun. Big toe, straight through the ball… over the bar. Kathleen Curran played in goal. She moved down to Kerry; she played with Dublin before that. They were well coached by Mick Fitzgerald. They had that Kerry ethos; they thought they were better than everybody else.

I felt the whole time we were getting closer.

There was one day in Tralee in 1989. We were three points down and we were through with two-on-one with the goalkeeper. One of our forwards passed it across to the other and the Kerry goalie intercepted it, kicked it down the field and they got a goal.

Instead of being level, we were six points down. That would test your resolve!

I felt very confident we were going to beat them in 1990 in Cappoquin.

We prepared really well and the likes of Ann Fitzpatrick and those younger players were flying. I felt we had a great chance. We also thought Kerry were slipping. They had won eight All-Irelands in-a-row... *This crowd can't last forever!*

They beat us 1-11 to 0-8. They beat us out the gate. They were just too good for us. It was a serious shock to the system.

The Munster president wasn't there. So, after losing by six points, I had to present them with the cup!

Kerry got so used to winning that they, inadvertently, forgot to bring the cup. Imagine that! We went looking for a shield down the town in Cappoquin. That may well have been a soccer trophy.

The rule was changed after that, and you had to bring in the cup a month in advance.

I remember walking up through Cappoquin and I felt so bad.

I sat down on the footpath outside the pub and Mari O'Ryan, my first cousin, came over and she said, 'I won't be playing next year... I'm moving away'.

She won an All Star that year.

Talk about being hit with a sledge. That took some getting over.

Jesus, I didn't know what to think.

The great thing about sport though is that there's always tomorrow.

New game, new championship.

A new start.

If you like something, it's an infection you get. Everything else seems secondary. It's probably a bad way to be but it just consumes you. Setbacks come and setbacks go but I just say, 'I'm not giving up'.

The players felt the same. They just wanted to win it.

ANY ADVANTAGE, I tried to get it.

In 1984, myself and Pat McGrath drove to Kerry to see the Kerry county final.

We waited until the game was on two minutes before we went in. Because we knew Mick Fitzgerald would be on the gate! He was the Kerry manager at the time!

There were two turnstiles.

Which one will I pick!

Mick Fitz was on the gate but I had the cap pulled down over my head and he didn't see me.

I remember we decided to bring Dolores Tyrell from midfield back to wing back. Dolores was the fastest player we had but she never played in the backs before. She had played all her football at midfield.

In Kerry, we had watched one of the opposition forwards. She was like lightning. I knew any of our two wing backs wouldn't stay with her.

We put Dolores back wing back and told her, 'Forget about everything else… you follow her all day long because you have the speed to handle her', and it worked a treat against that Kerry club in the Munster final. She never played at midfield after.

That's what we did. We went to see everyone playing if we could. I was always into that even when I was with The Nire under-21s. I was always doing that.

If I could get to see the opposition before a match, I thought nothing of driving down to Kerry.

I always felt it was worth it to make an effort to see the opposition. Arrive five minutes after the throw-in and be gone five minutes before the game was over. Slip in and out!

And say nothing!

I'd always wear a cap. A lot of games would be on in the winter time so I could have the scarf on, and the hands in the pockets.

Brigid was very good at going to see teams as well. Very good to make an assessment of the opposition and to see their strengths and weaknesses.

If we were playing the Kerry champions, I'd go in and get the Kerry paper. *The Kerryman* was delivered to Clonmel. You could buy it in Binchy's. It would have the details of the match.

Then I'd go up and see the match. I'd buy the Kerry paper for weeks beforehand and see how the Kerry championship was going along. *The Clare Champion* too, all those papers.

Anything to get an edge.

BALLYMAC PLAYED KERRY in a challenge game in September 1990.

They were getting ready for Croke Park and the final. We were getting ready for the Munster club. We won the All-Ireland club in 1987, '89 and '90.

They rang me.

We played them in Newport and we scored four goals against them. The first time ever we opened up their backs. It gave the team a bit of belief.

It certainly gave me a bit of belief.

We kept at it and at it. I don't know could we have ever recovered if we were beaten in 1991. It would have been very hard to come back after that.

A few young players came in. Everything was pointing towards the fact that we were getting better. We took five days off before the match, we finished on a Tuesday night. We felt really ready for it.

We used to fill up the bus with supporters going to Kerry in the 80s and 90s. We had a little core of supporters that travelled everywhere, no more than a hundred people. After 1995, we closed it down.

The whole thing got more serious. Team only.

People also travelled down in cars. Parents were always great. My mother came on the bus, as I said, with Johnsie Grant and my uncle Patie. A dozen people might get to travel on the bus.

By and large, people drove down in cars. They headed off for the day, some of them brought packed lunches. We'd be up the country and you'd see people pulled in at lay-bys having their sandwiches going up to see the match.

On the way, we stopped in Templeglantine. I walked around and looked at the players. Everybody was ready. Got to Listowel. Long grass on the pitch, and it looked as if the flags had been moved in a bit! The pitch was tightened up. It looked that way anyway!

Seventeen minutes gone, seven points down.

Getting beaten out the gate.

We put Noirin Walsh back in the backs; Olivia Condon came on and then we got a break. The ball came back off the crossbar and Áine Wall buried it.

Caitriona Casey got another goal.

At half-time we were ahead, 2-4 to 2-3.

I always felt we had the fitness if we could get our noses in front. We had the youth, we had the fitness and we had the hunger. Then, they got a penalty in the second-half and Marie Crotty went into goal.

They drove the penalty over the bar. We won by five (2-11 to 2-6).

It was a sense of relief when we won it. It was a mixture of joy and relief. I was shattered after the game; I didn't have the energy to jump around the place. I was totally shattered. Marie Crotty did an interview with Radio Kerry.

'For the last five years, we came to play Kerry… today we came to win.'

Big difference.

MARIE CROTTY WAS our go-to player for many years. She was the most skilful and the most talented player we had. She was the free taker.

She could play midfield, centre-forward or full-forward.

In the early years, she was the one who got the most scores. People looked up to her because when you wanted a free pointed and the game was in the melting pot and Marie Crotty had the ball in her hand, there was a fair chance she would put it over the bar.

She had a lovely way about her. She was very good with younger players, putting the arm around the shoulder and giving words of encouragement.

She also wouldn't be afraid to tell somebody, 'You need to step up here'.

And even from a management point of view, she'd tell you what she thought. She wouldn't tell you what you wanted to hear. We were lucky enough we had people like Bernie Ryan, Marie Crotty and Patricia Butler who would talk up which is good.

If they had something to say to me, they'd say it and then I'd make up my mind about it. Marie was a key player in every aspect, on the field and off the field. She was living in Dublin and she came down every weekend for training.

She set really high standards and the other thing was she was a very witty character. She'd always bring a smile to people's faces. She'd crack a joke.

It was a knack she had.

She had the perfect balance between being serious and having fun.

WE WENT BACK to the Bridge Bar in Ballymac and had a few drinks. We were late coming back. In the Bridge, you could stay late.

It was a pub I often visited over the years. Some good fun there.

There was always great banter when Waterford played Tipp.

People like Tommy Condon, Tom Moore, Tom Reynolds, John McGrath and Jimmy Butler. Tommy would have been an avid Tipp and Manchester United supporter.

Some great characters in the Bridge Bar. The owners, James and Catherine Lonergan were good supporters.

Some sensation in there when, on the sports news on the radio, we heard that… 'All-Ireland ladies football champions Kerry have been beaten by Waterford in a Munster final'.

It must have been on Radio 1. The score was given.

You'd almost pinch yourself. In those days, recognition was hard got. Media attention was very sparse. Coverage was very sparse. You were playing against the wind as regards media coverage because the only time you got coverage was when you got to the final.

I was at the All-Ireland final in 1993 – Kerry versus Laois, and Radio Kerry had nobody there and they rang me. I gave updates on Radio Kerry.

Updates on a team that had beaten us eight times! I did live commentary of the last five minutes.

That wasn't easy!

After that Munster final, the whole thing took a dramatic turn. A couple of weeks later, we played Kerry in a National League final; a replay, in Dungarvan. It went to extra-time. There was a men's match on first and a huge crowd stayed on. That game was a turning point as regards support.

We got much better support after that.

« CHAPTER 5 »

PLAYERS DROPPED OUT over the years because it was too serious for some people. To us, it was *serious* business.

One time, a player joined the Waterford panel from a different club. She was a good player but she was mad into socialising. I overheard Áine Wall saying to her, 'You're a very good player but if you want to play with us, you can't do those things'.

That player fell by the wayside.

ONCE THE WARM-UP was called, the chatter stopped.

At the start of every training session, I'd say to the players, 'What do we want from this session today?'

We'd work on one or two aspects every time. We might review it after training. If it went badly, we probably wouldn't review it.

We'd talk about it at the start of the next session.

If a drill isn't working, just stop it. Don't give 10 minutes trying to get it right, because it won't happen. I always believed there were only two or three things you could do in every training session anyway. It never lasted more than an hour and 15 minutes, although some players questioned whether my 15 minutes were a little bit longer!

In the runs we had, we put players of similar speeds together. We tried to create a competitive race situation because there's no point putting the slowest player on the team against the quickest player on the team.

We put huge emphasis on the ball.

Ninety percent of our training was with the ball and we played an awful lot of match situations. Because at the end of the day, the game is played with the ball.

If people were carrying the ball too much, a simple exercise I'd do was that I'd pick the slowest player on the panel and the quickest player on the panel. When I blew the whistle I'd tell the slowest player to kick the ball as hard as she could and the quickest player to solo the ball as fast as she could. When the ball stopped, which might be seconds later, I'd blow the whistle again.

Obviously, the person who was running was nowhere near where the ball was gone.

I'd call them back in and say, 'The moral of the story is nothing moves faster than the ball'.

Move the ball as fast as you can.

Move that ball.

Move yourself.

Move the ball.

We didn't just stand still after doing something, we moved on. That's where the seven-a-side came in. Constant movement, changing positions; we went from defending to attacking in seconds. It seemed to work.

I couldn't tell you what any other manager did but that's what we did. There was so much football in everything we did.

I'd ring every player myself. They'd know a week in advance when we'd be training.

I was a divil if somebody was injured. I couldn't wait until they were x-rayed. I'd have to be on it straight away. I'd have to know. I could ring somebody three times a day if they were injured, as if they were going to recover in four hours!

'How are you now?'

They'd be exactly the same!

IF YOU RAN a good show, if you prepared properly, if training was organised and if people were on time, the people who wanted to succeed easily bought into it. They weren't fools. They would know if something wasn't right.

I can tell you what helps.

Winning helps. If you're winning matches that's the biggest help.

I'm sure people weren't happy but it wasn't very obvious. If you were losing matches, that would come to the fore. If you were losing matches, people would find something wrong. It was a different mindset in those days.

Nowadays they're all looking for what Ger Loughnane said to me in the text after the Waterford hurling axe fell on me... 'Mr Magic'.

We always tried to bring on a couple of young players. With Waterford, we had the minors training with the seniors. I was the minor manager as well. Younger players playing with older players will improve the younger players and perk up the older players.

I'd always tell the younger ones, 'You're not in here to pay homage to those older players... you're in here to take their place, if you can'.

People had to train to get on the team, no favouritism.

If somebody wasn't playing well, they were taken off and somebody else was given a chance.

I think that helps.

I WAS ONLY late for a match once!

The clocks went forward.

The players were waiting for me at the Cross in Ballymac.

And I was never late for a match, they knew that!

I was big into people being on time because the idea was if people started coming late, everybody would be late. It was part of a discipline of a successful team, I thought.

The bus pulled up outside my house that morning!

It was a Waterford match; we were going up the country to a National League game.

The players often mention it!

USUALLY, I NAMED the team 20 minutes beforehand.

We would have been conscious of the team getting out to the opposition. It was a habit I had. We always kept things in-house.

If players were in doubt of their places, often I would mention it to them but I wouldn't release the team until we were in the dressing-room ready to go out for the warm-up. I felt that if we announced the team three or four days before a match and somebody wasn't happy, it could seep into the team. It also kept people on their toes.

The saving grace of the whole thing was the players loved to socialise together. They were great friends. There was no animosity between the players. Even in later years with Waterford, when Julie Torpey, Olivia Condon, June Whyte and many others came on, they got on really well. As a management we had to create an environment where people were happy.

If people enjoy what they're doing, they'll go to the well again.

I TRIED NOT to ever use bad language. You don't need to put 10 curses into a sentence. If someone is cursing at me, I just switch off from it.

I tried to put the onus on players to challenge players and very often ask a question of a player.

'Did you think that was the right thing to do?'

'Would you do the same thing again… if you got the chance?'

Ask questions of the players. Get them thinking about the game themselves rather than scream at them. Because screaming doesn't work.

They could take a rollicking at half-time. But I had to time it, or else they'd become immune to it in the finish. Every now and again you might raise your voice.

Like, I would be telling the facts of life fairly often. Not screaming and not using bad language. It just doesn't work. You don't need to do it. You might have one swear word in the whole conversation, but that's it.

If you have a hundred of them? I've seen other coaches and I've seen a lot of people at it. Roaring, bawling and screeching.

Players switch off.

With a team talk, you need to have a good punch line at the start, something good at the end and not go on too long.

I would have put a lot of thought into it.

I always liked to keep team talks fairly short. Most of the instructions would have been given during the week at training. It was only tidying up. A couple of minutes. People are ready to go out on to the pitch, they're a bundle of nerves and they're not listening.

You can't expect them to listen.

Everyone knew the way we wanted to play the game. We played a lot of possession football. We weren't into kicking the ball away, we wanted to keep possession and work the ball up the pitch and create space in front of goal.

WE PLAYED LEITRIM in the 1991 All-Ireland semi-final in Dungarvan. That was a massacre, 7-15 to 1-2.

We played Kerry in a league final after that and they beat us in extra-time. They beat us again! But that was no problem, we won the All-Ireland!

Laois were our opponents in that final. We were wary of them because they had beaten us a few times. They put it up to Kerry a couple of times. Laois were beaten in 1985, '88 and '90. They lost three finals and they fancied their chances of beating us. They were delighted to see Kerry gone.

As I've said, we always did very little in the four or five days before a match. We believed in being fresh. My father had a saying… 'You can't fatten the pig the day before the mart!' If you're not fit on Wednesday, you're not going to be fit for Sunday.

We asked the players to be honest with us if they were injured, or if they had a problem. Be straight with us. By and large, if you're honest with people, you'll get it back. From the Sunday before, we only really had one session.

And it would be a very light session. Then get up and go.

We'd always make the players aware of what can happen in a game. Things can go wrong, the referee can make a big mistake, the ball can come back off the post, people can get injured; we always tried to anticipate what was going to happen even though you can only prepare players for so much.

We also encouraged players to have a mind of their own and make their own decisions because it's a game of instinct.

Marie Crotty was great to call players aside. She was a real mother figure. So was Bernie Ryan.

I remember before an All-Ireland, Bernie sent out cards to all the players.

BERNIE WON ALL Stars at midfield, centre-forward and full-forward. When she was captain of the team, she had a habit of sending a note to all the players or doing something to bring everybody together. She'd be quiet but, a bit like Marie Crotty, she was really good with younger players. She was a leader in her own sense.

Marie Crotty had silken skills but Bernie had to work hard at her game. She was a good footballer however, and she could play in several different positions.

She wouldn't have the sense of humour Marie Crotty would have, but she was very much respected by the players.

Bernie was a person that you never had to say anything to. She was never found wanting for effort. She never missed training. She was very consistent; she was an eight out of 10 player every time she played. She mightn't be Player of the Match but she had a high level of consistency.

She was one of those people that you didn't have to worry about; you knew every day what you were going to get out of her.

Noirin Walsh would have been a general on the field as well. The O'Ryan twins too. We had five or six leaders. Olivia Butler. If you wanted a job done, leave it to Olivia and she wouldn't be found wanting. She would follow a person into the dressing-room at half-time if you told her, she would mark her that tight!

We really relished our first senior final.

We had players who had won three All-Ireland club titles, played in big games and played in Croke Park before. We played Laois a few times in the league and did well against them. We were confident going up; we felt we had the players to win the match.

We had six minors starting on that team.

Three in the backs and three in the forwards.

That was a lot, wasn't it? We won the minor All-Ireland that year as well and the under-16. Fiona Crotty was on all three teams and she was on the club team. She won four All-Irelands in the one year and started on every one of those teams.

That can never be done again.

ANYTIME WE WENT to Dublin, we travelled up the night before. We stayed in the West County Hotel if it was available. We always tried to go to the final of the seven-a-side the day before. We left home at one o'clock, got to Dublin about five, went to see the final of the 'Sevens', came back and had something to eat.

We always had a chat the night before, nothing major though.

On the evening before or the morning of the All-Ireland final, we always went to Mass. There were two churches near us at the West County. Everybody would arrive in their tracksuits. It was something we always did. When the priest got to know us, he used to give us a mention. It was nice.

In those days, most people went to Mass anyway.

I don't ever really feel pressure before a game. No matter how well you prepare, the morning of a match you always feel that you've left something out. You wonder have you covered everything. In later years, I learned that you can't cover everything… 95 percent is covered.

On the morning of a match, the players would all be up early because they couldn't stay in bed. I wasn't too bad; I was better to sleep then than I am now!

Every year we went to St Vincent's for a kickaround the Sunday morning before the match. I think Marie Crotty had a contact there, she was working in Dublin.

ANN FITZPATRICK HAD a calf muscle injury before the 1991 final. I didn't think she was that bad until she contacted me on the Friday evening before the All-Ireland. We went over to see a physio in Clogheen called Pat Flynn but he couldn't come with us to Dublin. He had been doing a bit of work for us.

In those days, there wasn't as much emphasis on physios as there is today. Now, everybody has a physio. I rang the Waterford county secretary, Seamus Grant.

'I'll give you the name of the best physio around, a fella called Billy Kelly.'

So, I rang Billy Kelly. You know when you're trying to impress someone?

'Billy… Michael Ryan manager of the Waterford football team.'

I'll never forget what he said.

'Oh you lucky fella!'

Tongue in cheek!

'Billy,' I said, 'I have a problem.' He told me he lived in Mooncoin and I said we'd call into him on the way.

We went down and he looked at it. 'She's bad enough,' he said. We thought we only had one injury at this stage.

He worked on her. He said that if it was looked after properly she would play.

'Would you come with us?' I enquired.

'I can't.'

He faithfully promised us that he would come up later that night.

THE MORNING OF the match, Pat Grant told me that it was lashing rain. The last thing I wanted to hear.

Then, Billy discovered that we had another injury… Regina Byrne. Billy took Fitzie and Reggie out on the lawn for a fitness test.

They're fit!' Billy proclaimed.

A mighty cheer.

'Laois are in trouble,' Marie Crotty said.

We chose the same dressing-room that Kerry used to have. Martina and Geraldine O'Ryan insisted that we take it. We were anxious to get on the pitch early. I met a smartly dressed official, Jim Bannon from Modeligo, Dermot Bannon's father! *Room To Improve!* He opened the gate for us.

We spoke for two weeks about getting a good start. Laois had lost three All-Irelands, we couldn't afford a bad start.

We put a lot of work into the game-plan in the couple of weeks before that final. Áine Wall was at full-forward and she had lightning pace. We wanted to make it a one-on-one between Áine and Connie Conway. Connie was the Laois full-back, a tough cookie now! She didn't collect prisoners!

We cleared everybody else out of the space. The two corner-forwards went out to the corner flags. Give her 30 yards in front of goal.

Get the ball to Áine Wall.

Jesus, it worked a treat.

She got 3-3 in that final.

I've never seen a better forward than Áine Wall. I know people will say Cora Staunton and she was an incredible player, no question about that. Áine changed her game as she got older. In her early years, she had no meas in points, like, she was only interested in goals. She was goal mad and she got loads of goals.

I can't get over that she hasn't been covered on *Laochra Gael*. She was one of the greatest players of all-time. She was the best finisher I worked with, male or female. She wouldn't be the greatest team player but some of the best forwards are not fantastic team players.

She was exactly what we wanted.

The best strikers are a little bit selfish. She'd go for the goal and be prepared to take five lashes to get there. In later years, she got 2-2 in 1992, 1-5 in the 1994 final and five points in 1995, all from play.

In an All-Ireland final, everybody is going to have their spell. You're not going to dominate the game.

The big worry was Sue Ramsbottom. She was a serious player.

She scored 3-5 out of 3-7. The difference between the two teams I felt was we had better forwards as a unit than Laois. They had Sue.

If you closed her down to 2-3, that was holding her! She was that good. Ten years later, I was in the Laois dressing-room with Sue. Funny old world isn't it!

Our goalkeeper, Patricia Butler got a clobber, she had a badly swollen knee. It was a 50-50 ball; she went for it and they crashed into one another. Lord have mercy on her. Martina O'Ryan started kicking out the ball because Patricia couldn't kick it. We had to put Ann Fitzpatrick in at corner-back.

Áine got great ball. Everyone was flying. You know the day when everybody plays well. Crotty and Bernie were on top all day long at midfield. The pace and movement in the forwards was very good. We got five goals. Geraldine O'Ryan was a very intelligent player. Caitriona Casey would put the ball on a sixpence, right or left foot. June Whyte also played her part.

We always kept our noses in front. We were comfortable coming up to the final whistle. Áine got the last point. 5-8 to 3-7.

There was relief but there was also a lot of happiness and joy because there was nine years gone into it. We were at this since 1982 and we had so many setbacks along the way. We were favourites in the final because we had beaten Kerry.

Joy and relief.

Everybody was let out on the pitch in those days. My mother would always run out on the field. The players' parents. The likes of John and Ann Crotty, Mari O'Ryan's mother, Johnsie, my uncle Patie, Caitriona Casey's father.

Anybody who had a relation, they were out on the pitch!

The twins' mother, Maureen O'Ryan, Mick and Lizzy Byrnes, Larry and Kathleen Walsh, and June Whyte's mother, Kathleen. The parents of the players and the relations of the players would always be the first out.

No restrictions, everybody was let out!

It was a big deal because we won it. A first new winner in 12 years.

A load of telegrams came to the hotel.

There was a telegram from Mary Robinson, who was President at the time.

It made the six o'clock news on the television, and there were clips on the radio. Nothing like the coverage today.

We came back to Dungarvan.

It was the first time they had the stage in the Square, and then we went to Ballymac. I don't know where the players ended up; some of them didn't come home for three or four days! They went to the schools and they went to one another's homes.

They were great at that.

They would always gang up and stay together. They weren't massive drinkers. They loved to sing and loved to party. A lot of them wouldn't have had boyfriends.

Football was number one, football was number two... football was number three.

« CHAPTER 6 »

They're the proud protectors of arguably the longest winning sequence in Irish sporting circles. Dubbed 'The Invincibles', the Ballymacarbry ladies footballers wrote themselves into the history books last Sunday when they won the All-Ireland Senior Club Championship for a seventh consecutive year with a 17-point victory over Parnells of London.

– John A Murphy, Irish Examiner, December 7, 1995

WE WERE GOING all year round.

After the All-Ireland, there was no rest for the majority of the panel. They were back training with Ballymac on the Wednesday night to prepare for a Munster semi-final the following Sunday against Beaufort. We won it 7-15 to 1-4.

The season used to end on the last weekend of December and we played National League again in February. We'd be off for maybe six weeks, and then go again.

After the 1995 All-Ireland win, Pat Grant jokingly said to Cleona Walsh in Doocey's at one o'clock in the morning that we had club training the following night. Cleona and her sister Sinéad were serious defenders, as were Ann Dunford, Martina O'Ryan and Regina Byrne.

'I'd go training this minute,' she replied.

That was the attitude they had.

We'd be back training on the pitch for the club 48 hours after bringing home the Brendan Martin Cup and everybody would be there. That was the attitude.

It was all about attitude, desire and hunger.

WOMEN WERE MORE dedicated than men, more committed, mentally tougher, didn't give up as easily and were more loyal to one another. If women are pulling together, they can move mountains.

I did come across men's teams that had a great attitude. I came across a good group of lads in De La Salle, a good group of lads in Mullinahone, and the Waterford team with Justin McCarthy.

Maybe it's their attitude to life or their philosophy on life. They were less likely to get carried away after winning.

They didn't look for excuses, they just kept going. Such fight, such willpower and such desire to succeed. That's my experience, other fellas might tell you differently. If you had an argument with a woman, it's very hard to win it.

They don't throw in the towel very easily.

I don't see any towels in women's boxing. They don't throw in towels!

WHEN WE GOT a taste of success, we were determined to drive it on as much as we could. I always enjoyed the final whistle.

The last couple of minutes, when you know a game is in the bag, is a fantastic feeling. When we got there, we enjoyed it so much that we wanted more. The only way we could have more was to work harder, and get better. Move with the times and move on from a training and preparation point of view.

We had suffered so much and seen so many disappointments; the idea was to make sure we do everything we can that this doesn't happen again.

I often had long chats with Brigid Grant about this. Brigid was incredibly sharp as regards players. She seemed to know when somebody was coming to the end or when somebody wasn't doing it 100 percent right. We often bounced things off one another.

Brigid would often say to me there's not much left in this player or that player is losing interest. We were always evaluating who was ready to take the team forward and who was ready for the next challenge. Like the Grand National, the next fence had to be jumped and if you didn't, you were out of the race.

I often think nowadays the game is gone too serious and fellas like me are the reason for that.

I would have been responsible for people giving a huge portion of their lives, people like me and other coaches around the country. We would have been responsible for pushing training up from one night a week to two nights a week, to three and four… and maybe five nights a week.

I did what I felt we had to do to win.

If there was an edge to be got as regards fitness or preparation, we did that. We were probably ahead of our time as regards preparation for ladies football.

The one thing I will say is that everything we did we did with the ball.

I'm happy enough about it because I think players enjoy working with the ball. Ninety percent of our training sessions were with the ball. What I've seen, in the last 10 or 15 years, is that an awful lot of stuff is done without the ball.

Running, running, running… running.

At the end of the day, it's about kicking the ball over the bar. I wonder how much time is spent at that part of the preparation.

The county team was nearly the club team. Caitriona Casey joined Ballymac because there was no other club in West Waterford. She was from Clashmore. We won our first All-Ireland club title easy enough in 1987. The following year we paid for that.

We were caught below in Callan by a very good Adamstown team. We never really got going. It was a bitterly cold day. Absolutely freezing. We were probably overconfident and walked into a haymaker, but that's unfair on Adamstown because they were an excellent side. They deserved to win it.

We had to start again. Sinéad Walsh came on the team and a couple more young players came through and we were up and running again.

We went unbeaten from 1989 to '96. I remember Áine Wall was taken off after scoring six goals in the first-half of a Munster final against Beaufort. 10-7 to 3-3. We hammered teams.

We won the All Ireland Sevens in 1987, '88, '89 and '90. Four in-a-row. In two of those years our second team won the Plate (1989 and '90).

The 1991 All-Ireland club final against Rochfortbridge was a tight one. 0-9 to 1-4. We beat them in four All-Ireland finals (1989, '91, '92 and '94) and the semi-final in '90 in Tyrrellspass. One of their players always tells me how lucky we were!

You're telling me we were lucky?

We played them five times and we won the five games. Her husband was the secretary of Westmeath County Board. Small world isn't it, as I later managed the Westmeath hurlers.

Apart from that, it was plain sailing most of the time. In 1997, we hammered the Wexford champions, Shelmaliers in New Ross. They sportingly formed a guard of honour as the players left the pitch.

Some of those scores in All-Ireland club finals were just ridiculous.

1987: Ballymacarbry 4-10, Hollymount 1-2.

1989: Ballymacarbry 0-9, Rochfortbridge 0-3.

1990: Ballymacarbry 4-9, St Grellan's 0-3.

1991: Ballymacarbry 0-9, Rochfortbridge 1-4.

1992: Ballymacarbry 3-8. Rochfortbridge 1-2.

1993: Ballymacarbry 2-12, Crettyard 1-2.

1994: Ballymacarbry 3-12, Rochfortbridge 1-6.

1995: Ballymacarbry 4-12, Parnells 1-4.

1997: Ballymacarbry 5-10, Shelmaliers 0-3.

1998: Ballymacarbry 2-15, Portobello 0-8.

We were miles ahead. That group of players was just unique.

WE LOST DOLORES Tyrell and Claire Williams to cancer in 1993.

That was tough going.

Dolores died in hospital in Dublin. For someone who was so fast and so fit, and for that to happen. She played wing back in the All-Ireland junior final in 1986 and captained Ballymac to the All-Ireland club title in 1987. She was a really consistent player and great to train. Lightning fast.

By the time we became a real force in senior, she was coming to the end of her career. She retired in 1991 and died in '93.

She was very quiet but deeply respected by everybody. She had a funny sense of humour. Somebody told a joke and 20 seconds later Dolores laughed! She played a big part in Ballymac's early success and establishing Waterford as a serious force.

Noel Murray, who was chairperson of the Ballymac club for many years, mooted the idea of the club donating a cup in her memory, for the All-Ireland

Club Senior Championship.. We did several fundraisers, including a sponsored walk, and presented the cup to the association.

It was first played for in 1994.

I remember there was a lot of tension in the dressing-room before that final. This was the Dolores Tyrell Cup, our captain when we won our first All-Ireland in 1987, and we wanted to make sure that Ballymac would be the first winners of that cup.

There was no way we could lose that final.

Claire Williams played in goals for us.

Prior to Claire coming along, a lot of outfield players played in goal. She was the first really natural keeper we had. That was her number one position. Unfortunately, she died very young.

To lose two players, both to cancer, in one year was tough going. For our club. For our players.

For the families of Dolores and Claire.

I HAVE ONE big regret about it.

In 1996, we were down to play a Munster final in Clare against Cooraclare on a Saturday and a National League semi-final against Monaghan on a Sunday.

We had a couple of girls who couldn't get off both days from work. We could have played that club game on the Sunday and let the county go.

We took a gamble. We travelled to Cooraclare without two or three players.

The referee?

OH MY GOD!

I won't forget his name but I won't mention his name either!

I'll never forget it! He had a shocker!

I'd been suspended 12 years before so I let it go!

All day long. All the 50-50 calls. There were some terrible decisions. We were beaten in extra time. 4-10 to 2-15.

Our first championship defeat since 1988.

We had to play the two games on the same weekend but maybe we should have played the club game and forgot about the county. But we didn't do that because we were carrying the county anyway. We encouraged as many players as possible to play with the county. We couldn't get enough people on the county panel. We always felt it would improve them. We had subs on our club team who were subs on the Waterford senior team. That's the way it was. We lost the league semi-final to Monaghan as well. It was up in Clones. We drove from Clare to Dublin and stayed in Dublin.

Then, I met Tom Moore in Doocey's.

'And ye got beaten yesterday!'

'... how did ye manage that?'

PART TWO

Home Sweet Home

« CHAPTER 7 »

IN THE SUMMER of 2000, it was obvious that my mother, Maureen was going downhill.

Two years earlier, she got an aneurism outside the church in Newcastle and was brought to hospital in Clonmel. She made a recovery but she never again came to see us play.

I visited her in St Joseph's Hospital in Clonmel in September.

I brought in a football in a plastic bag and I was talking away to her. There was no movement. I spoke to her for a while about this and that, and I couldn't get any reaction.

'Have a look and see does this make a difference,' I said to the nurse.

I took the football out of the bag and held it up with one hand in front of her face.

She nodded and smiled.

The nurse couldn't get over it.

She was in a semi-coma.

She passed away on January 2, 2001, three months later. She had been in decline. When she was sick and I knew she wasn't going to make it, I'd always pray that it wouldn't happen when there was a match on. She didn't let me down!

There were no matches on!

My mother was always on the team bus in the early days. When Waterford or Ballymac were playing, as I've said, there was some room for spectators. She travelled everywhere. She was always in the second seat from the front. When we'd be going at eight o'clock, she'd be ready at seven.

My mother was a fanatic, never missed a game. She travelled the length and breadth of Ireland following teams and tore her hair out on a regular basis. She was a very intense person; she was very passionate.

She really enjoyed sport and it was a very important part of her life. Whatever passion I have, and I have a fair bit of it, I definitely got it from her.

MY FATHER HAD absolutely no interest in sport.

He was known locally as 'Tom Scully'. He did his own thing. He was a man who liked a pint. Horses, not horse racing, were his big passion. He went to fairs like the Tallow Horse Fair. He travelled around with Mickey English buying horses.

Absolutely no interest in sport.

He wouldn't watch it on television. Even when we were playing in Croke Park... no interest. Absolutely none.

He'd always say the best of luck. He'd wish you luck but he had no interest in the game. He certainly wouldn't be at the Cross waving a flag! There was a session when we came back and he enjoyed that alright. If he didn't have any interest, he didn't have any interest and that's the way it was. His brother, Patie went to all our matches, on the bus with Johnsie Grant and all of those. They went to all our games. Travelled to Croke Park and travelled everywhere. That was the other side of the coin.

In 1989, when Tipp won the All-Ireland, he was in Melody's pub the following day and lads from Newcastle came over. They were probably looking for somebody to get a rise out of. The aul fella and Mick Guiry had a good few pints drank.

They were slagging him but sure he didn't take any notice. Someone told him the following day, 'Jesus Tom, you let those Tipperary fellas get away with murder... you never opened your mouth'.

The following Friday, there was a funeral on in Newcastle.

He met the two lads.

'Jesus, ye're great fellas coming over to Ballymac slagging me about the All-Ireland. Myself and Mick Guiry... we didn't even know there was a match on!'

That sums him up.

No interest. Absolutely no interest.

He worked with Willie Trihy in the building, worked with Clonmel Foods; he was always tearing with horses, working in the wood taking out timber. Lots of different things. He never tied himself to a career. He spent the longest time in the building with Willie Trihy and worked with Séan Guiry and myself as well.

He had a very bad accident back around 1960. He was coming back from Clonmel one evening on a horse and cart. I think he lost the reins; he was after a few pints. He climbed up on the horse and the metal spike around the horse's collar went in through his head. He was fighting for his life for a while.

He never drank til he was 27 or 28, which is funny because he really enjoyed his pints. In some ways, he was larger than life. He was the centre of attention in the pub. It was in an era when there were a lot of great characters going to pubs. They used to meet on a regular basis, drink a lot of beer and have the chat.

They weren't too interested in the world or current affairs. They were interested in local affairs. He never missed a funeral. His life was very local. Most of his life was spent within 10 miles of his home. He was in Dublin once or twice, and he was in England once.

He never really travelled.

He did enjoy his pints, no question about that. Even when he was very sick and he left home for the last time, me and my sister, Chrissy brought him down to the hospital in Ardkeen.

'We'll be back in Doocey's won't we... for one?'

He never came out of it; he died two weeks later.

We always had a lot of banter, though I wouldn't say we were best buddies. We got on alright. One thing he was big into was saying, 'thanks' and 'please'. It was a great lesson in life.

He was a very plain fella who liked the craic. He liked playing pranks on people. He had a good sense of humour, once it was going his way!

I WAS CLOSER to my mother because she was interested in the hobby I had. We would have spent more time together.

My mother was the complete opposite to my father. She was a Pioneer all her life. She was a couple of years older than him. She received her golden pin for being a Pioneer for 50 years.

Her big thing was the ICA.

She was in the ICA for years and years and years. The ICA and the Tidy Towns. She started the Tidy Towns in Ballymacarbry. Herself, Nora Doocey, Cait O'Keeffe, Nellie Norris, Pat Melody and a few more. It started off in the early 70s. They were her main hobbies as well as sport.

She had a good core of friends around the village. She always milked the cows at home. We had a small farm, 26 or 27 acres. She loved work but she liked her trips away with the ICA and the ladies football.

When a day came to go out, she loved that. She'd be looking forward to it for weeks, maybe months. If the team played bad, she'd never criticise. She never cursed but she used to say,

'What the frigging hell happened?'

That was her big phrase.

She had a couple of tragedies in her life.

She lost her brother when he was 43; he died after an accident in Clonmel. I remember her brother and her brother-in-law died the same Christmas, both 43. Her brother-in-law was killed in a car accident in England. That was a poor Christmas.

She'd fight on her back for her own.

She was totally biased as regards her own family. If she liked you, she'd die for you. If she didn't like you, she'd tell you about it.

That was her, there was no beating around the bush. Straight as a die. Straight down the middle. She'd back you to the hilt. It didn't make a difference if you were wrong, she'd still back you!

She was happy at home.

She loved her home life.

We couldn't have asked for a better mother; she was a great woman.

I AM A home bird.

I never would have lived anywhere else other than Ballymacarbry.

I love the village, I love the people.

I love the GAA, I love ladies football... I love Ballymac.

When I'm away for a weekend, I always want to get back. It's a special place. We have an awful lot going for ourselves.

You're only 10 miles from Clonmel, 15 miles from Dungarvan, 20 minutes from Cahir… and motorway all the way to Dublin.

I wouldn't have picked anywhere else to live.

I GREW UP in a house at the back of Melody's pub in Curtiswood.

It was almost in the woods. The real Curtiswood, I suppose. It was like a little village. A couple of hundred yards from the pub, there were three houses. Eddie Coffey was there, Lar and Bridgie and Paddy Moroney, and our house. Three little houses. The pub and the shop were just down the road. Then we moved into a cottage down in the village and then I built my own house in 1980.

Back in the 60s, there were no airs or graces.

Times were tough enough. We were like everybody. We had no more or no less than anybody else. We only had a small house. Three bedrooms.

One of them was actually a parlour turned into a bedroom. Myself and my twin brother Willie were in one room. The house was small, it was compact but it was warm, there was always a good fire going.

It was a thatched house and there was a yard around it. A barn where the spuds were put in, a cow house and a little piggery. That's all there was really.

We didn't have a car; my father never drove.

He probably owned a bike. He always had a horse. He never had a problem getting a spin, someone was always there. If he went down to the road, he'd get a spin straight away.

He always got around.

When I was 10, I was asked to go out and live with my grandmother, Mary Mike. My uncle Kieran was a county councillor and was often away from the home. I lived there for three years in Knockalisheen. I remember waking up at seven o'clock in the morning, bringing in the cows and milking three cows by hand. Going up to Bill Ryan's and getting the spin into school. I've hated cows ever since.

My grandfather, Michael O'Ryan died in 1950. He was my mother's father and Kieran's father. He was involved in the county council as well. He was in jail during the troubles, very actively involved in the fight for freedom, like a lot of people were in those days. He died in 1950 to cancer.

Kieran took over in the county council in 1955 and served for 54 years; he was the longest serving councillor in the country when he stepped down.

When the cows were milked on a summer's evening, we'd go play matches. I remember playing games above in Bill Ryan's field. John, Jim, Paddy Joe, Anthony Ryan, myself and anybody else who could catch a hurley. To us, they were like an All-Ireland final! That was 1965 to '68.

My grandmother was a very straight woman. Like all grandparents, she was strict but she was fair as well. You wouldn't be stepping out of line. I remember going out to Healy's every night, next door. They'd have a radio. Tommy and Willie were there, and Andy, Peg and Mary and we'd have a chat. We were lucky enough Kieran had a television; there weren't too many televisions around at that time.

Then when I came back to Curtiswood, Lar Moroney had a television.

At the end of 1969, we moved down from Curtiswood to a cottage in the middle of the village and there was a telephone kiosk across the road. In those days, very few places had phones so a lot of people stopped at the coin box to make a phone call.

It was a hive of activity.

In those days, there was Melody's and Doocey's pubs, there was St Patrick's hall, and Doocey's also had a small hall further down with mini dances. In the village that time, there wasn't a footpath. Our house was built and there was no other house built for years and years and years. It was dangerous walking up the street, it was an accident waiting to happen.

Building the central school in 1972 was a big deal because five other schools closed down. There were protests everywhere. The Nire people didn't want their school closed down, and Bennettschurch didn't want their school closed down, and a local man, Paddy Phelan lay down in front of a car in protest.

It was just a coming together that made sense. In those days, sections of parishes were parochial. Nobody wanted to give an inch. Thankfully, common sense prevailed and history has proved that it was a good decision.

To see the way the village has developed in the last 20 years is incredible with the community centre. Five guys came together at a meeting; Séan Guiry, Richard Guiry, Danny O'Rourke, Pat Ryan and Mick Fenton who was the chairman. I had only a small part to play doing a bit of fundraising.

That community centre is an incredible building in a country place. You have two different halls, one with the artificial surface, another which seats 220 people;

the gym, the sauna, meeting rooms, a hostel. That's a monument to those five men and all the people of the parish that rowed in behind it.

Ballymac is a lovely village to drive through, the Tidy Towns have looked after it really well. There's also community housing for the old folks. They have made a village out of what was almost a hit and miss.

« CHAPTER 8 »

I'M TWENTY MINUTES older than my twin brother Willie and he has never caught up!

August 9, 1955.

There was always fierce rivalry between us. Always.

We were polar opposites.

We didn't look alike; he was a little bit taller.

I liked school, he hated school.

We started going to the High School in Clonmel and he went mitching one day in the wood. Pat Melody was the local teacher and he asked me where was Willie? I told him he was very sick. Lo and behold that evening, Pat met my mother below in the shop.

'How is poor Willie? I hope he's okay.'

'How do you mean?' she says.

'Isn't he at home… sick?'

All hell broke loose!

There was holy war when we went home!

I got away with a verbal but he got a bit of a trimming.

We both went to the High School for a year and then he changed to the Tech. To meet the bus, I had to walk down to the Tech. In December 1969, I was running and I slipped. My leg hit the bottom of a wall. I knew I was in big trouble. I broke my leg.

I was brought to Cashel hospital in an ambulance.

We had no car in the family. The message got home to send somebody up for me. Willie said that he'd ask my uncle Kieran. He took a horse out to Kieran's house. We always used to have horses at home.

He went out the Nire road thinking he was Lester Piggott! He was flying out and when he turned at Knockalisheen Bridge, the horse fell and his leg went under the horse and he broke his leg as well!

Both of us had our left leg broken at the same time!

Kieran collected me in Cashel, went from Cashel to Ardkeen Hospital, dropped off Willie and brought me home!

Why we went to two different hospitals, I don't know!

We both recovered. He had a wooden set of crutches and I had a metal set under my arm. We were living in the cottage below the Post Office in Ballymac. We were both on crutches for Christmas 1969. We used to have races up and down the road on the crutches!

Imagine that! We were always so competitive.

There was always a battle.

Willie was a mad Dublin fan. He was a Dublin fan because I was a Kerry fan. Polar opposites again! Brian Mullins was midfield for Dublin and he put the nickname on himself. Everyone calls him Mullins now. Everyone in Ireland.

I remember watching the 1963 All-Ireland football final down in Melody's where there was a television. Dublin and Galway. We were lucky enough to have a radio in our house. Michael O'Hehir was the big thing. In 1982, when Kerry were going for five in-a-row, I was sitting on a chair at home and I actually hopped the chair off the ground, and broke one leg of the chair! I was so disappointed.

I wanted Offaly to win an All-Ireland but I wanted Kerry to win that one!

I was in Croke Park in 1971 as well when Offaly won their first All-Ireland. Funnily enough it was football finals I went to first.

I was always a fan of Kerry and Kilkenny. My first hurling final was 1973. Limerick and Kilkenny. The day Ned Rea got the pushover goal for Limerick! About four fellas pushed him over the line!

You wouldn't get into the dressing-room now.

You wouldn't get onto the pitch now. That's how much everything has changed.

In those days, you could get into the dressing-room after the match. In 2018, when I was with Westmeath, we weren't allowed out on the pitch for a walk in our runners half an hour before the Joe McDonagh Cup final.

KEEP OFF THE GRASS.

Yet U2 can sail across the grass!

Amazing!

I WENT INTO the Kilkenny dressing-room in Croke Park after the match in 1973 and got a hurley. There was no bother getting into the dressing-room. Kilkenny were beaten and all the activity was around the Hogan Stand and I drifted into the dressing-room.

A fella called Liam 'Chunky' O'Brien, who was midfield for Kilkenny, sat down and I asked him for a hurley. He was so depressed after losing the match that he gave me the hurley and I had it for a good few years.

I brought it home and won a county minor medal with it!

John Morgan asked me for a loan of it and played in the county intermediate final with it. I'll never forget it. The boss was spliced. Two sections spliced together and a double hoop on it. It's long gone now.

IN CURTISWOOD, THERE was a garden with a clothes-line in it.

That was our pitch. Twenty-five yards long.

The clothes-line was at one end and we had two makeshift poles on the other side. We hammered the ball at one another and that was it. That was where we played our sport.

Willie was a better hurler than I was but he didn't have the interest. I was better at football. I was an average hurler. He could have easily played senior for Waterford. He was part of the under-21 team that beat Clare in a Munster final against Ger Loughnane and Co. He was 19. He played in goal.

He played away for a bit. He gave it up for a while in about 1978. Then, we played Touraneena in the county final in 1979 and he came back and played midfield. That was more or less the end of it.

Pat is my youngest brother, he was always up to mischief. They were thatching the house. The ladder was left up. Talk about health and safety! We were above having our intense game of hurling. The old fella came home from work.

Pat was about six and climbed up to the top of the roof. The old fella came up and went ballistic.

He went *ballistic*!

When he called us down first, we didn't know there was anything wrong.

Like, Pat could have been killed off the roof.

We came in with our hurleys. He grabbed the two hurleys and put them under the pot and the fire was on. We were starting to panic. Hurleys were a big deal for us.

'Mullins' gave him a bit of cheek and he ran after him. I grabbed the two hurleys while they was gone!

They were black but they were intact!

A club league started off and I bought Pat a pair of boots. I was working Saturdays with Willie Trihy on the building site. We played a match down in the Millfield and he scored seven or eight points.

He never played after that. No interest. That's the way it was.

Willie was a top class badminton player, as was my sister Bernie. He was slim. I played myself as well. We played in the All-County League. We were Division 2; we played Division 1 for a while. We travelled all over Waterford and to Kilkenny, New Ross and Youghal as well.

Billy Doocey and Father Mick Byrne started the badminton team. We had four teams in the club; divisions 1, 2, 3 and 4. Bernie was the best one of us.

My eldest sister Marian was one of the founder members of the Ballymacarbry ladies football club in 1970. She didn't play an awful lot after that now. My second sister Chrissie played for a while before she went to England.

They both went to England.

Marian met her husband over there; she came back in the early 80s.

Chrissie married a Mayo man, Pat Horkan.

Willie went to England as well. The three of them were in London. They came home to see all our matches in Croke Park. Bernie was playing, of course.

I wouldn't say we were hugging one another but we always got on fairly well.

Bernie married Brendan Duggan and went to live in Greystones when she retired from playing so the only one left at home was Pat.

Chrissie came back from England to be closer to my mother and look after her. They built a house in Castlereagh and she stayed. When she came back she didn't expect our mother to pass so soon.

She looked after my father in later times. She was a nurse originally.

Chrissie is the motherly figure in our family.

Marian came home and went teaching. Her husband died in 2016 after a battle with cancer. A really lovely fella called Michael John Shinnick. A real gentleman.

Michael John was very witty. In 1990, Cork had won the hurling and they were going for the football. Michael John wouldn't have been an avid GAA man. He went into his local pub above in Glanworth and someone asked him was he going to the match. 'Of course, I wouldn't miss it for anything,' he replied.

This fella pipes up, 'How in the name of Jesus did you get a ticket? My wife is washing the jerseys, selling the tickets… doing all the work for the club and she can't get a ticket… and a fella like you can get a ticket.'

He was very annoyed.

The following Sunday, in Croke Park, Michael John is sitting down and who comes in and sits two rows in front of him? His friend from Glanworth!

He looks back and he sees Michael John. He's absolutely fuming!

The two teams come out and Michael John says, loud enough for your man to hear him… 'Which of the two teams are Cork?'

Your man went crazy!

Stone bananas!

Pat was Pat. Pat was very witty, very funny, never short of an answer. He could throw in a few choice words as well! No big interest in playing. Chrissie played ladies football with Ballymac. She was a Liverpool supporter.

Marian was a founder member of the club and played a bit as well, but she emigrated to England where she lived for several years.

Willie was a really good badminton player; he played badminton for Munster. Himself and Bernie were serious badminton players.

Bernie was the shining light in our house as regards sport. She captained Waterford to a senior All-Ireland and won three All Star awards. Every honour in the game. In 1992, she captained the club to the Munster and the All-Ireland, and captained Waterford to the National League, the Munster and the All-Ireland. Five cups in the one year.

MYSELF AND MY two brothers would always have a bit of banter. We wouldn't leave a thing go. Willie is an Arsenal supporter; he was a season ticket holder for a while. Pat is a United supporter and I'm a Liverpool supporter! Chrissie and Bernie are Liverpool supporters as well. And Marian supported all of us.

I remember buying a ticket in Chadwick's in Clonmel. I bought a pound ticket and I won a trip to Wembley to see Liverpool playing Arsenal in the 1986 Charity Shield, and a hundred pounds spending money and tickets to the show, *Les Misérables*. Some weekend for a pound!

We flew over from Waterford.

'Would you like to see the cockpit?' the pilot said to me.

He brought me in to the cockpit and everywhere I looked there were loose nuts and bolts! And they were rattling!

'What I'd like now is to get this plane back on dry land!' I told him.

He started laughing!

A few of us also went over to see United and Liverpool at Old Trafford. Back in 1998, it was around the time of the Good Friday Agreement; we got the trip from Chadwick's because we were customers.

Myself, Séan Guiry, Liam Long, Micheál Tierney and Seamus Ryan. We were in the middle of the United fans. The first thing that struck me was the gigantic stadium.

Michael Owen scored.

I jumped up and punched the air! The next thing, this fella behind me piped up.

'You Scouse bastard!'

Micheál Tierney turned to me.

'Sit down or you'll get us all killed!'

As a 15 or 16 year-old, I became chairman of the youth club. Johnny Coffey started it; he was secretary. I liked the idea of being chairman or some way active and trying to lead. I don't know if lead is the right word but I always seem to end up in those situations anyway.

We had a play going one time, a boxing sketch, and we went down to Carrick-On-Suir. We were probably having a few pints at the time. Mick Sullivan brought us down in the hackney car. There were a few acts on before us so we went to the pub.

We missed our turn!

Johnny was secretary and he'd be a meticulous type of man, and he got wind of it. Johnny launched a serious investigation but didn't poor Mick die in the meantime, so that was the end of the investigation.

We did set dancing as well.

Monnie Hallanan had a set dancing team. We danced in a few county finals in Scór but I wouldn't say I was Fred Astaire! Behind the hall was a handball alley that was in disrepair. Where Pinewood factory is now, we put up a volleyball net and marked down a court in Donovan's field as it was called that time. My father was renting the field and he wasn't very impressed! We went down to play our volleyball and our net was rolled up and thrown at the railing and we were told never again to go in there!

That was the end of our volleyball days in the youth club!

It goes to show how scarce resources were in those days.

There was nothing much happening.

WHEN I WAS 10, Tommy Healy and a few lads used to come up to our place for St Patrick's Day. Tommy gave me a sup out of a large bottle.

In no time at all, I was langers. We were afraid of our lives of the guards down in the village. Hagan was the guard. Tommy told the story years later that I went to bed and woke up after a while and I went down and said, 'I'm not afraid of you now, Hagan!'

I was never a big fan of drink anyway. When I took the pledge in school, I took the pledge for life. I remember when they said to take the pledge until your 18, I remember distinctly using the word *life*.

I never drank again until I was 19.

Nineteen years, three weeks and three days. When I had my first drink, I said that I'm breaking that pledge now... *19 years, three weeks and three days.*

The guy that bought me my first pint was Gerry Crotty, and he also bought my father his first pint. He would have been a cousin of my mother's. My father drank a good few pints more than I did! We went into the pub on a Friday evening coming home from work. I often used to go in and have a mineral.

Gerry asked me would I like a pint, and I said I'd chance one pint. It took me a couple of months to develop a taste for it!

It was never a big issue in my life, thanks be to God.

WE'D SIT ON the wall of the Cross at Melody's and hope that someone would bring us somewhere. If there was anything on, we'd all jump in a car. If there was space in a car, we'd be in it. That's the way life was.

I always went to matches. I went to All-Irelands when I was 15. I went to my first match in my uncle's car aged eight.

If there was a match in Dungarvan, I'd just go.

If there was a match in Cappoquin, I'd just go.

If there was a match in Clonmel, I'd just go.

I went to Munster finals. I was in Fitzgerald Stadium in 1987 when Tipperary beat Cork in the replay.

I always went to matches. That was my big hobby.

I got friendly with John Morgan and Willie Prendergast about 1971 or '72 and I went to matches every Sunday with them. The following year Willie Prendergast took us over. We went up to Flower Lodge in Cork, which is now Páirc Uí Rinn, when Waterford FC won the league in 1972. Somewhere at home I still have Dave Kirby's jersey.

John Morgan got Alfie Hale's. Waterford needed to draw the game to win the league. They were 2-0 down with 11 minutes to go and they scored three goals in the last 11 minutes. They won the league and they threw their jerseys over the railing.

I remember grabbing one, pulling it from somebody else. It got caught in the barbed wire and it ripped a small bit of the jersey. I've had it at home for years.

The following Sunday they met in the cup final and Hibs beat them 3-0. Miah Dennehy got a hat-trick. I often went to Kilcohan Park with Billy Doocey to watch soccer matches. Waterford won the league six times in eight years.

Anytime I got a chance to go somewhere, I went. It was a long week, like. Especially to see Alfie Hale and Johnny Matthews. Peter Thomas was larger than life. You could hear him roaring over the crowd…'MY BALL!' Bobby Charlton played there one day.

I loved going to Clonmel in the early 70s because Mick Connolly and Jim Wall were playing with Waterford. I was going to the High School at the time and Waterford and Tipperary were in Division 1. Big crowds.

We often went in to see Clonmel Commercials playing Ardfinnan or Kilsheelan. That was war! On Sunday evenings, there'd be big games on in Fraher Field.

There was no *Sunday Game*. The only match televised was the All-Ireland final. We had Michael O'Hehir on the radio… lucky enough to have a radio. That was the sum total of growing up.

Always something to do or somewhere to go.

WE WENT DOWN to the Millfield any chance we got. We played soccer on the Millfield which was sacrilege in those days!

I started playing when I was 16. Richard Power had a soccer club going. Frankie Connolly got me involved. We were in the Tipperary League and travelled on a bus every second Sunday. We could be playing above in Templetuohy.

We won Division 2 and there was a social in Hearne's Hotel in Clonmel. I drove out the mountain road afterwards and turned the car over on its side. I only had it two years. I paid £1,500 for it, which was a lot of money.

A blue Datsun 1200.

9910ZU was the number of it.

I turned it over on its side, alright. There was only myself and my girlfriend at the time, who ended up being my wife, in the car. It went up on the fence and gently rolled over.

It wasn't spectacular.

A fella across the road called Gus Kearney came out, pushed it back and pulled it into his own house.

Tis some feeling to wake up the following morning and your car is gone!

My brother Willie was a mechanic now and he went down the following day to look at it. A write-off!

My £1,500!

I wouldn't accept that so I brought it into a panel beater and he fixed it for £140!

« CHAPTER 9 »

I LOVED NATIONAL school, I really *loved* national school.

I remember going to school in Bennettschurch. The first day I went, we walked down the boreen to Melody's and there was a bus. Dinny Hyland was driving the bus, the Clonmel to Dungarvan bus.

He'd give us a spin up an odd day if it was wet.

We had to walk to school after that. The world was a different place then. We walked up through the wood, out on to the main road… walked up by the grotto… and the same thing home again in the evening. Brought our lunch, a couple of slices of bread; that's the way everybody was.

No such thing as tea. You had a bottle of milk going with you because everybody had a few cows at home. The milk certainly wasn't pasteurised but it didn't do us any harm.

I HAD A great time in national school and that's where I played my first matches. Bennettschurch had a team and we played in the North Waterford League. We won it a couple of times. Paddy Joe Ryan was captain the first year we won it. I was only nine or 10 and I played in goal.

I was a very poor goalkeeper! The second time we won it I was midfield. Fellas like John Cliffe, Tyler Walsh; a lot of them didn't ever come through. Willie was a really good hurler and played in an All-Ireland under-21 final against Kilkenny.

Did I tell you, I *loved* national school?

There was only 30 or 40 pupils in the school and only three or four in our class. Great days. I loved history and geography.

There were two teachers in Bennettschurch. There were two rooms and there was a partition, so if the teacher was missing, you could pull back the partition. One day I was in third class, the partition was opened up and the teacher was Tom Dalton.

He gave us something to do as he was doing history with the fifth and sixth classes. He asked something in history and I've told you I *loved* history, and nobody in sixth class knew the answer. Then he asked again…'Does anybody in fifth class know?'

He was getting frustrated and he was getting loud.

'Does anybody in this room know?'

I put up my hand; I was only in third class, and I answered it. I was delighted with myself. I went out to play and I got a right good hammering off the sixth class boys.

That put me back in my box!

I never really enjoyed secondary school. The Christian Brothers insisted on teaching history, geography and maths through Irish. I wasn't a big lover of Irish. Funnily enough my daughter is an Irish teacher now!

It was a different story.

I was away from home, left at eight o'clock in the morning and wasn't home until half five on the bus. The High School in Clonmel was a good school but I probably didn't have enough interest in it. My best days were in national school, loved it.

ONE BANK HOLIDAY Monday in 1969, I spent my first day on a building site. I was 14, and my father was working with Willie Trihy and I asked him for a summer job. I got it and that was manna from heaven.

I remember the first time I caught a trowel. We were doing Willie Healy's house, and they couldn't get block layers. Willie Trihy bought a couple of trowels and he said, 'Here, grab that and off you go'.

I picked it up fairly quickly.

Six days, a fiver a week. Nice money in those days. Not a lot of money but nice money. Then I asked him for Saturday work and they started building the school in Ballymac. That gave me my interest in the building.

When you were earning money in those days, it was hard to do anything else. I would have liked to have gone on to do PE teaching but my Irish wasn't good enough. In those days, you couldn't do anything if you hadn't honours Irish. That's the way it was. I applied to a college in England called St Mary's College in Strawberry Hill in Twickenham in London but when the figures came back I just couldn't afford it.

I did my five years in secondary school, did my Leaving and got through it no problem.

I had a job so I decided to serve my time in the building with Willie Trihy. Laying bricks and laying blocks. We worked down in Dan Desmond's house, I'll never forget it. Willie Healy and Mickey Whelan. Digging a foundation by hand. I was 14 at the time. Then, we worked on the school in Ballymac after that. Started at half eight and finished at half five. Four on a Saturday.

I liked the building. In those days, it was pre-health and safety. That doesn't mean there were fellas getting killed every minute, but there were no big regulations.

We never did silly things. No one got seriously hurt.

When I was in San Francisco in 2014, I couldn't believe that I saw two or three storey buildings along the side of the streets and no scaffolding, and Mexicans on the roof. Ireland was a bit like that 50 years ago.

Now, all of that has been tightened up. In those days time didn't make a big difference.

'There's no bit gone out of tomorrow!'

That's what Tommy Healy used to say.

It was great fun. You'd be out there trying to boil the kettle in the middle of nowhere in a green field, sitting around having your lunch. My mother would always make my lunch. Sitting around the fire having the craic and, then, quickly enough, the roof would be on the house and we were having our food inside… it was like a hotel!

MYSELF AND SÉAN Guiry set up Ryan & Guiry Builders in 1979 and we're still here 41 years later. We had both worked for Willie Trihy. It was a good idea because I was a block layer and he was a carpenter. He'd lay a few blocks with me and I'd give him a hand with the roof. Then we started employing a couple of fellas and it grew from there.

We covered Clonmel and Dungarvan, down as far as Stradbally. Fifteen or 20 miles from Ballymac... Cappoquin, Dungarvan, Stradbally, Kilmacthomas, Carrick-On-Suir, Clonmel.

We had 15 fellas on the books in the peak times. We could have had another 15 as sub-contractors. We could have 30 people working for us in the boom times.

That quietened down again and now we only have a couple of fellas working for us. The wheel has come full circle.

Séan is very witty, very funny. There is a never a dull moment with him. He is a great worker and a good organiser. I've never seen him in bad form.

We played together. Decent player. Good footballer. He scored the winning goal for Fourmilewater in the county intermediate hurling final in 1989. I was coaching the team. He managed The Nire team. I don't know would The Nire have ever won a championship only for he took over that team. Even though he didn't do any coaching himself, he got in people who were good at it, like John Phelan.

We had a lot of locals working with us.

The craic was great in those days. Every Monday morning we would always be talking about matches. Monday evening we went for a few pints, Friday evening we went for a few pints. Train a couple of times during the week, go to a match Sunday and have a few more pints!

We would have done up a few pubs, doctor surgeries, smaller industrials. We knew our range and we knew our depth. We weren't going to build the Taj Mahal!

Pinewood Healthcare were always very good to us, and GSK in Dungarvan. We got a lot of work from Pinewood over the years. It's right beside the Millfield where we all started. It is a great employer and sponsored the ladies football team as well.

There was never a shortage. People were always looking for somebody to do a job. We were young lads, we had energy, jumping up on roofs was no bother!

From 1990 on, it went crazy.

Everyone was shouting, everyone wanted everything done.

Houses got bigger. In the middle of a job, people made it twice the size. There wasn't enough workers to go around. It seemed to me the banks were throwing money at everybody. I heard stories of guys who went to get a mortgage for a couple of hundred thousand and the banks said, 'Why don't you take another 25 thousand and buy a car?'

I heard stories of people having mortgages confirmed by text message.

It couldn't last, but nobody thought it would go as fast as it did. When you stop and think about it now, the whole Irish economy was dependent on the building. Whereas nowadays, there's more IT and pharmaceutical companies and there's a better chance of it lasting. In those days, it just couldn't last.

Nobody could do anything to stop it. I mean, building houses with five bathrooms!

You can't keep five bathrooms busy at the same time! It reached a stage in the 2000s where the tarmac had to be done, the lawn had to be manicured, the garage had to be finished, the satellite dish had to be on the roof. It was a different world.

We went through a recession in the late 80s. Things were bad in Ireland. Somebody asked me to build a pier. I called over and he said, 'I never thought anyone would come and build a pier.' Six months later, he gave us the house to build.

I feel sorry for young people today who can't get mortgages. I know people now who are paying more on rent than they would on a mortgage. They just can't get a mortgage. My daughter was renting in Dublin and was paying more for one room in Dublin than a mortgage was costing in Clonmel.

Incredible!

NEVER SAW THE 'Book of Common Sense'. Somebody should have written it.

We were okay but a lot of people weren't that lucky.

We were never out of work, we kept tipping away. Pinewood and GSK kept us going. Elsewhere, everybody stopped building. Health and safety and all those issues came into it. It reached a stage before the crash where you would be paying five or six people who didn't lift a block.

The person drawing the plans, the quantity surveyor, the insurance, the health and safety. They all had to be paid. The prices were crazy because someone had to pay, and that was the poor customer.

Everything came back to earth with the recession.

Everybody suffered, everybody lost and we were no different. Everybody had to adjust. We went down to five or six people and now we have two and we're happy with that. The whole thing changed.

The customers we had kept coming back if they were doing an extension. Word of mouth was a big help. We were never out of work.

The fact we were both involved in sport was a help as well. I went to Westmeath, like, to manage them! Séan understood I had to go away at four o'clock. Séan is into sport.

As I got older, I wasn't going to be laying a couple of hundred blocks a day. We got in block layers and we did the handy bits ourselves. Tidying up or organising or driving the van to get stuff.

I wouldn't be jumping up on the roof every five minutes!

IF I HAD my time back, I'd like to have gotten into something like sports journalism. Writing wasn't a big thing for me but I've always enjoyed working with a microphone.

But that's the way it fell for me. Looking back on it, I've no regrets.

IN THE 90s, I started doing video commentaries. I did The Nire county final in 1993 when they won their first senior title against Dungarvan. It was a wet day in Cappoquin. As the half-time whistle blew, the case of the Dungarvan first aid person opened and all their stuff fell out in the wet.

I remember saying on the commentary… 'Tis all going wrong for Dungarvan right now!'

About three months after that, I met Tom Cunningham, who played for Dungarvan and for Waterford in 1959. He saw the video; his son Fergal was playing, and he said for a fella whose team was playing in a county final, it was a very fair commentary. That was nice to hear.

I always tried to be fair anyway. So that kicked off my video commentary career. If you did one, people think you're Jimmy Magee! If you get the name wrong, on the radio it's okay, nobody will see it. It's hard to get everything right.

If you're doing the television commentary, if you're not sure you can fob it off. I did the next four or five finals and the intermediate hurling final in 2001 but after about 2005, people didn't want the commentary anymore.

WE HAD NO RTÉ 2 in Ballymac for years.

Imagine that! Six of us set up a committee to bring RTÉ 2 to Ballymac. We put a mast up in Deerpark and beamed it. We got Tom Kelly, who was working with RTÉ, to give us a hand. The signal was beamed into Ballymac and transmitted around the village. One channel up to that point and poor reception!

Then we had the BBC coming in from a mast out in the Nire but after six months it was taken away. I was always onto Séan Casey in Dungarvan to see if anything could be done. Then I met Dermot Kirwan. He asked me to do a few commentaries for him.

I remember going to Kerry to do a Rathgormack game in the Munster Club Championship. And I remember going to the RSC in Waterford one night to do an underage soccer international. He would make a copy of the tape and show it Monday night. He stood in the General Election in 1997 and I went canvassing for him. Even though I have no interest in politics! He got 4,000 first preference votes, he was nearly elected!

I've always enjoyed working with a microphone. I got a phone call from WLR to do a commentary on Mount Sion and Patrickswell, Kieran O'Connor got held up. When you're always talking to teams, it doesn't bother you.

A commentary is an extension of a team talk.

I would have liked to have done more media work over the years. I enjoy that end of it. It happened in bits. I did a few bits for RTÉ on the *Saturday Sport* programme with Joanne Cantwell; I got to know Joanne through ladies football. I was involved with Dublin in 2010 when they won the All-Ireland and Joanne was presenting the medals.

Joanne played for Dublin when I was managing Waterford and she said, 'My memory of you is coming into our dressing-room after giving us a mother and father of a hiding… and telling us to keep going!' I was on *Championship Sunday* with Paul Collins on Today FM as well. I've done hundreds of functions.

THEN I STARTED being asked to say a few words at funerals.

I call it an unfortunate privilege. It's a privilege to be asked but there's someone suffering. That's tough. Especially 'young' funerals.

You look down the church and everybody is hurting. It's okay to talk about somebody who is 85 because you can tell a few good stories and it's almost a celebration of their life, but we've had some tragedies. To see people so hurt is tough.

I've been doing it over 20 years. What I've learned is that if you can make it a story of their life and tell a few funny things that happened, you can bring a smile to people's faces. If you can do that, it might ease the tension and bring back a few good memories.

I've probably changed the way I do it over the years. Humour is a great thing. A smile without making it a laugh, if you know what I mean. You don't want to be disrespectful in any way. You have to think it through and be careful what you're saying in public.

Thanks be to God, I never had any issues.

I always treated those things as speaking to one person.

Make it a one-to-one.

Try to forget about the crowd. As you get older, you don't even notice those things. You need to be up for it though. Because if you're not up for it, it won't happen. I'd go through it in my mind. If I was saying a few words at a funeral, I'd meet the family and have a chat. You can't expect it to flow without having a bit of homework done.

I remember one time the priest asked me to give out communion and I said, 'I don't think I'm a good enough Catholic'.

Then he asked me to do the readings.

'Sure, if I give out communion and do the readings… you may as well stay at home!'

We both had a good laugh over it!

« CHAPTER 10 »

MY WIFE CATHERINE was into sport as well.

She lived a couple of miles out the road and she used to go to matches. Even though there was a few years between us, she used to be on the school bus going to Clonmel.

She went to the Tech in Clonmel with my sister Chrissie. They were good friends. They were more or less the same age.

In those days, I might be in Jim Wall's car going to matches or whatever.

She played and was on that Ballymac team in 1975 that won the first county championship. She was centre-back. She was always going to matches. We hit it off. In those days you might be going to a dance with Jim Wall or Paddy Joe Moore. It wasn't a planned thing, it just happened.

We got engaged in 1979, and married in 1980. The function was on in Kilcoran Lodge Hotel and we had 125 people at it. In those days, it was a huge wedding! We went on honeymoon to Tenerife. It was a big thing at the time.

We started building a house in 1979 and we always wanted to live in Ballymac. My father gave us a site. Catherine was working in the glass factory in Dungarvan.

She played up until Michelle was born. She went back after that for a little while at junior. She is big into it and loves to go to matches. She takes photographs and keeps scrapbooks. That's a hobby of hers; it's a good job she does because a lot of stuff would have been lost.

Catherine is very supportive. The first team I managed was 45 years ago and I'm still involved with the Ballymac ladies. When I was with the Westmeath senior hurling team, I was up there over 40 hours a week. I'd leave home on a Wednesday at half four and I'd get back at half one in the morning. Wednesday and Friday.

I'd go up Saturday evening at seven o'clock and I wouldn't get home until seven or eight o'clock Sunday evening. I often went up for gym sessions on a Monday as well. I drove to Mullingar 600 times.

I think it's about 180,000 miles.

Overall, she has been a great support to me, no doubt about that.

She'd have an opinion on players and games; she'd be sharp. If she thought I made a mistake as a manager, I'd hear about it. She wouldn't be afraid to tell me.

'Why didn't you do this?

'Why didn't you do that?' Sometimes she'd be right!

I always listened.

Once somebody was sober, I listened. If somebody was drunk, I couldn't hack it. I'd just walk away. Usually that person wouldn't open their mouth when they were sober.

EVER SINCE THE kids were able to walk, they were kicking a football around our place. They were all great to train.

Michelle started in the forwards, moved to the backs and then moved back up to the forwards again! She won a minor All-Ireland playing left half-back. She was very good to deliver the ball and very good to read the game so we put her in the backs for a couple of years at underage. When Michelle was about 11, she wasn't very tall. Suddenly she shot up and she's six feet tall now. One day, we played her in the forwards and she got a couple of goals and we pushed her back up again.

Sinéad, from the time she got on the team first, could score. She won the Golden Boot in intermediate football in 2010. She was on The Nire boys under-14 team that won a Western championship. She was only 14 when she played her first senior match. She played under-14, under-16, minor, junior and senior for Waterford... all in the one year!

She always wanted to be on the scoresheet. She preferred goals to points, she loved scoring goals. We used to have a mark at the gable end of the house and she kicked the ball at it. Michelle and Louise would have been kicking the ball to one another but Sinéad was that bit younger so she was trying to hit a spot with the ball, trying to improve her accuracy. Shane was the same way.

They were always behind the goal kicking back the ball. Michelle tells a story about hoping there'd be an odd number so she could join the game or join the drills. It often happened.

Everything in our house revolved around sport. There was always a match, there was always a training session. It was something we always did and it was something we always enjoyed. Looking back on it now, we got a great return from it. We had fantastic times all over the country.

Michelle, Louise and Sinéad put so much into winning the intermediate All-Ireland with Waterford in 2015. That group of players lost in 2010, lost in 2012 and eventually won it in 2015. The whole family was there that day. Michelle wasn't starting and I thought she should have been starting.

The manager, Pat Sullivan has explained it several times about how he wanted an impact coming off the bench but I thought she was playing well enough to start. If you're not starting an All-Ireland final, it's hard to get over, but she did. They played really well on the day. I remember Michelle McGrath, who would be a no-nonsense defender, put in a serious collision. If you wanted to go to battle, the first player I'd pick every day of the week is Michelle McGrath.

In fairness to Pat, he did a very good job with them. He had Noel O'Connor, who would have been with the Cork team under Eamonn Ryan. They were in a good place that day and were a good bit better than Kildare.

After losing two, to win that one was great. For all the players, not just our three. I really enjoyed the last couple of minutes of that game when you knew they were going to win it. Linda Wall was the captain. She had been there so long and she had so many disappointments. The emotion she showed on the steps of the Hogan Stand, the tears in her eyes, that's what this is all about. I love genuine emotion.

Louise and Sinéad sang *Dungarvan My Hometown* after the cup was presented. Deirdre Nagle did it in 1998, Deirdre was a good singer. I don't know who came up with the idea. Sinéad is a decent enough singer and Louise wouldn't be the best singer on the planet but she'd be a willing participant!

Louise was an eight out of 10 every day. She played in the backs, in the middle and in the forwards. She did the simple things well and she was a great team player.

According to the players, she was one of Ballymac's best ever captains. She did things to bring the players together. She would organise a trip or a day out.

Being a nurse and a teacher, she knew how to handle young people. If they had problems or needed reassurance, she was good at that.

Louise also has a great sense of humour, brilliant one-liners. Always positive. In our family, you can always go to Louise and have a chat about anything because she's a good listener. She has a soothing effect on everybody. If something needs to be done, Louise goes and does it. Your best health insurance policy, all the simple jobs even without being asked. A very unassuming and a very generous person.

She was due to get married to Ian O'Regan last July, but had to postpone the day due to Covid.

IN 2010, I missed my three daughters playing an All-Ireland final in Croke Park.

I was in charge of De La Salle and they had a quarter-final against Tallow fixed for the same afternoon.

There were extensive representations to the Waterford County Board to change the match to Saturday. The Ladies Football Association even got onto them.

It was laughable the offer that was made. They said that they would switch the time of the game so I could see the game on television. They were going to change it to half past three. So, I would watch the game on television and have five minutes to go into the De La Salle dressing-room!

Unbelievable!

That was tough to take. That should have been changed.

In fairness, the De La Salle chairman, Seamus Quirke said, 'Look, if you want to go to the match, you can go to the match'.

I said, 'I took this job… I won't go to the match'.

The previous year, Tipperary changed it when I was Mullinahone manager. I was with the Dublin ladies so I asked Mullinahone to put an email into the Tipp County Board to ask could we play our quarter-final on a Saturday. Tipp acceded to that request.

A year later, Waterford put on a game at the same time that I had three daughters playing in Croke Park.

That was an absolute insult.

De La Salle won the game easily.

Waterford were beaten by Donegal and I went to Dublin straight after the match. I was involved with the Dublin ladies as well, they won the senior on the same day. Dublin won, De La Salle won and Waterford were beaten. So, I drove to the Waterford hotel and I ended up going to the Dublin party that night.

Michelle, Louise and Sinéad were very disappointed. The biggest day of their lives in sport and this to happen. They weren't surprised because if I commit to something, I commit to it and that's it.

It was needless. It just didn't have to happen.

It annoyed me.

IT WAS A big deal to win the Division 2 final against Kerry in 2019.

Waterford were brilliant on the day. I'd been at the semi-final against Cavan; Michelle scored a hat-trick. The football they played was fantastic.

They weren't just playing anyone, they were playing Kerry. We had so many battles with Kerry over the years in my time. Kerry had beaten us in four Munster finals, and beaten us in a lot of major games before we got the hang of it and beat them.

Virtually everybody on the Waterford team had a nine out of 10.

I was thinking to myself at the final whistle… *This could be Michelle's last big day out in a Waterford jersey.*

I went down to the gate and the steward didn't want to let me in.

'There's nobody stopping me today!'

In fairness to the gate man, he let me in.

She caught my eye straight away. Brendan Moran from the Sportsfile photo agency captured it on camera. I didn't even know he was there. It was pure delight and satisfaction at seeing a Waterford team play so well, play football as good as the glory days. The standard of football that day was super. To beat Kerry in a final is always good.

I spoke to them a few days before that league final down in the Gold Coast. The Waterford manager Ciaran Curran asked me would I come in as a surprise speaker.

If you're speaking to any group of players, you have to get their attention in the first few sentences and you have to finish strongly. I spoke about what it meant to play for Waterford. I went back over my experience, and I spoke about all the disappointments we had and the way the players overcame all that, kept going and it turned for them.

SHANE WAS ON the Waterford minor hurling panel and the under-21 panel. When he was young, Fourmilewater played a championship match in Dungarvan and they were a point down with two minutes to go and he got a ball 30 yards out.

Jesus he's going to put it over the bar.

He took on his man.

I could have killed him!

The next thing, he stuck it in the back of the net. Then he got the puck-out. Another point and the game was safe but he kept going again, and got another goal.

He was always a good player. His confidence has improved in recent years. He always had the ability and the attitude; a great trainer and great to do the gym work.

He captained The Nire to win the championship in 2014. He was only 21 and they beat Stradbally. The Nire hadn't won it in six years. They won it well. Conor Gleeson was exceptional on the day. Shane was the leading scorer in the championship that year. He was always a decent speaker. That wouldn't be any bother to him. That was a special moment. We embraced on the pitch afterwards, another embrace!

He played football with Waterford for a couple of years and played Fitzgibbon Cup with WIT. Westmeath were doing a training camp in Abbotstown when he got a goal in Wexford Park for the footballers in the All-Ireland qualifiers. That's the story of my life!

There was a fantastic photograph where they were all sitting along the quay in Dungarvan. It reminded me of that famous photograph in New York with the steelworkers sitting on a girder. Lunch atop a Skyscraper. Someone wrote a piece in the paper a few days later that it restored their faith in sport that after winning something, the players could go out, have a drink and enjoy themselves.

Shane got a call-up from Derek McGrath for a month but that never came to anything and then he got the call from Liam Cahill.

It was an opportunity he was craving. He started against Tipperary in the league but got injured after 20 minutes.

All four of them have given us brilliant days out.

GERALDINE O'RYAN TELLS a story.

We were playing a league semi-final against Monaghan and she was doing her Leaving Cert. I insisted that she had to go to the game and she didn't get a minute after going up. She reminded me of that years later!

Claire Ryan tells a story that one day she wasn't playing well and I told her at half-time that she was coming out wing forward and her next move was out beside me!

Now, I believe in trusting the management because I've seen too many people trying to instruct players. They don't know where they are if they're getting loads of different instructions.

All I say to them is every day is a different day. Justin McCarthy often said to Paul Flynn and Eoin Kelly, 'Every free is a different free'. You have to treat it like that.

Shane took the frees for The Nire for a year or two and the only advice I ever gave him, he never took it! That was to kick the ball off the ground. I can't understand why more fellas don't kick frees off the ground. I always took them off the ground, you had no other choice in my day.

You have more control of the whole thing. So, the only advice I ever gave him taking frees, he didn't take it!

For Sinéad and Michelle up front, movement was the key. I would often say that to them… 'Don't be running in straight lines… change the course of your run… change direction'.

I wouldn't say I gave them an awful lot of advice over the years but the only thing I would have said to them, over and over again, was… 'Don't come off the field saying I could have done that. Put all you have into it while you're there'.

Another thing I say to a lot of players is this… 'Your playing career is very short, you'll be a spectator all your life when you stop playing… get the maximum out of it'.

MICHELLE AND LOUISE went to America on holidays in 2008.

They hired a car and drove from San Francisco down to Los Angeles. It was mighty, but our hearts were in our mouths at home! Particularly their mother!

A photograph came back of Michelle driving and Louise in her sunglasses and her two feet out the window!

From the time they were born, we always tried to go on holidays somewhere every summer.

We went on a Sunday evening after a match and we were back Saturday afternoon! That's what we did!

We went to Dingle a few times, and Clonakilty.

When you're going away with a young family, it's almost chaos because you've four small kids and there's only seven years between them. As they got older, we went to Spain and Portugal. When they get to 16 or 17, they want to do their own thing.

That's life. They were very enjoyable days, those holidays.

In 1998, we went to Galway, out to Clifden and stayed in the Station House. We were coming back from that holiday and this caravan ahead of us had a poster on the back of it. We drove up close to see what it was. It was an old battered caravan.

Obviously, this family were doing the same thing that we were.

'WE'RE THE O'NEILL'S… THE JONESES' ARE MILES AHEAD!'

That was the sign on the back of the caravan.

It was something that always stayed with me about the importance of being yourself and not trying to be something you're not.

« CHAPTER 11 »

I HAD MY own ball for taking frees.

I was only 19 when I became free taker for The Nire.

At the start of every year, The Nire would buy two or three footballs and I'd take one of them home. I'd go down to the field then and practice frees with that ball. Before the game started, I'd hand that ball to the referee so I'd know that I'd be taking the frees with my football.

In those days, very seldom did you lose the ball during the match. Very seldom. There weren't many footballs around.

Every match that I could, I'd always give the ball to the referee.

I only had the letter 'N' on it because if you had 'Nire' you could be caught out. No one ever cottoned on to it!

I was always trying to learn. I was always trying to get an edge.

I remember The Nire played Abbeyside in Cappoquin on a windy day. I was only a young fella. Tony Mansfield from Abbeyside said to somebody, 'What way are we playing?'

'We're playing with the wind.'

He pumped up the ball.

At half-time, he let the wind out of it. When you think about it, it makes sense. If you're playing with the wind, the ball is going to travel further.

I was accurate, I could kick with both feet. I was a half-decent free taker but I was no Maurice Fitzgerald! I was an okay footballer. I didn't tear up many trees. But I was a better footballer than I was a hurler.

I always practiced frees and penalties. I did a lot of practice but my range was only about 40 yards. I didn't kick 45s. I never took a free out of the hand because in those days, it wasn't allowed.

Around the mid-70s the GAA changed the rule around penalties. Prior to that, a penalty was only for a foul inside the small square. Then, they introduced the bigger penalty box coming out to the 13 metre line. There were a lot of fouls in that area early on and a lot of teams gave away penalties so I spent a lot of time practicing. I went down to the Millfield with Thomas or Brian Norris kicking back the ball, they were only five or six years of age.

I had a good run.

The first 12 penalties I took, I scored them but I missed the thirteenth! It was a league game inside in Dungarvan against Ballinacourty. I remember it well. I struck the left hand post at the dressing-room end. It was a Thursday night.

We came back out to Ballymac that night and we had a drink in the pub.

Somebody said to Tommy Healy that I missed a penalty. Tommy wouldn't have gone to a lot of matches but he would have an opinion on everything!

'I wouldn't blame him!' he said.

I thought he was going to praise me!

'I'd blame the fellas that let him take it!'

I HAVE A SCAR on my right arm.

It was an intermediate hurling championship game in 1980 against Tourin.

Jesus, I thought I was dead.

It was an accident. Myself and Ollie Wilkinson were both pulling on the ball. The hoop of the hurley caught my hand. I saw the hoop just before it happened. The whole hoop opened, I could have been killed, like.

It wouldn't have been a bad place to die would it? Fraher Field!

I ran over to the sideline and someone rang the doctor. The doctor came over in the car. The man who looked after me only had one arm. There were no First Aiders to be seen! He just consoled me and told me to put my hand up over my head to try and stop the bleeding.

Jimmy Stacey was the doctor who stitched me in Dungarvan.

THE BIG REGRET is that I didn't have more days with Fourmilewater.

We won the minor 'A' hurling title in 1973 with Willie Prendergast. My brother was on the intermediate team in 1973, he was the only minor on it. The rest of us were subs. We played Ballydurn in the county final in Walsh Park.

Fourmilewater were shocking now. Absolutely shocking! I was a sub. I was walking up the tunnel in Walsh Park… in those days there was wire over the tunnel.

One fella says to the other fella, 'Jesus if the team are that bad, what must the subs be like?'

I couldn't help but laugh!

We were beaten by Clonea in the 1977 intermediate final.

Hammered. 3-7 to 0-4.

Myself and Willie got sent off. Another lesson learned!

I told the referee to open his eyes and he wasn't impressed. It was in the last few minutes and the game was long over. Willie and his man pulled on the ball and the hurley broke halfway up and the ref gave a free against him.

He stuck the hurley down on the ground.

Straight red. The two of us got straight reds. As I wrote in the Fourmilewater club history book, we had the dubious distinction of being sent off in a county final.

Fourmilewater should have got to a senior hurling final. They should have beaten Dungarvan in the semi-final in 2012 but they took their eye off the ball. That's the lesson I learned a long time ago from Touraneena.

I OWE TOURANEENA a great debt.

In 1979, they beat us in a Western intermediate hurling final. We thought we were going to win that game. If we looked at the bigger picture, we would have seen that they had four players on the county panel. They hurled us off the pitch in Dungarvan.

Lucky enough, we got a chance in the county final to do something about it, and we did. I was never complacent about any match since.

In 1979, when we won that intermediate hurling title, we had five selectors and three of them were playing. Tony Doocey and Paddy Grant were the only two who weren't playing. Myself, Mick Connolly and Pat Halley were on the field. In those days, the captain was automatically a selector.

There wasn't a posse of fellas going around training teams. It was nearly always the players who did the training. That was the way it was in those days. Outside coaching was a rarity.

Training wasn't well attended. Gerry Coffey, John Morgan, Mattie Whelan, Séan Guiry, Denis and Jackie Hogan, Pat and Michael Halley, Jim Ryan and Philly Harte were always training, they would never miss a training session. We also had fellas who mightn't turn up until the week of a match. In a country area, unfortunately, there wasn't much we could do about it. If you look back on the period when that happened, there was no county championships won. It was only in the years where a special effort was made and people took it seriously, like 1979, 1983 and the 90s, that we won matches.

You show me the man who doesn't train and I'll show you that same man with no medals.

I WAS SENT OFF in minor football in Touraneena in 1972. We were playing Ballinameela and we had a good team. A row broke out and two of us got sent off. The referee probably picked the two nearest fellas to him.

The spectators came in from outside the pitch. There was war!

Everybody was in the row! I remember Tommy and Willie Healy coming in, everyone!

We were well ahead, the match was stopped and the ref went home. Brendan O'Brien from Abbeyside, Seamus O'Brien's son. I can still see him walking out the gate!

It came up before the Western Board and the Western Board chairman was Kieran O'Ryan! My uncle! He fired out the two teams. We were winning the match easily; we had a team good enough to win it out.

A championship thrown away. A great lesson in discipline!

I played until 1990. Seventeen seasons playing adult football.

In 1974, The Nire got through the losers group into a senior semi-final. We never before won a senior semi-final. We were three points up against Affane in Fraher Field.

Jim Wall, who was Munster full-back at the time, got sent off. Himself and Pat Denn got sent off. We lost the game by three points. We were in Doocey's that night and we were saying…'We'll win it next year!'

MICHAEL RYAN CHAPTER 11

Richie Foley was on the team and Richie would be a supreme pessimist, now. 'None of us will ever again play in a semi-final!' he said.

The Nire didn't get back to a semi-final for 13 years. I was the only fella still playing, so he was nearly right!

We played Affane in the first round of the 1983 intermediate championship and my brother Willie got married the day before. We were terrible, I don't know how we won the match. Eventually, we got to the Western final and we beat Ballyduff Upper and we were terrible again. I remember the supporters around the Cross that night in Ballymac. They said it was the worst team that ever left the Cross.

We got some time to prepare for the county final and we trained really well. Tony Doocey supplied shorts and Melody's supplied socks. We wore blue shorts and yellow socks. To my recollection, it was the first time ever The Nire wore blue shorts.

It was my own idea.

Do something different. It makes a team look bigger and physically stronger. If I had my way, Waterford would wear blue jerseys instead of white.

White is a ghost's colour, you don't notice it. You notice the red of Cork. It's something I did with the ladies football team in 1998. We had a clash with Monaghan so we wore blue, and we wore blue for a good few years after that.

I always felt that a team looked more intimidating in a strong colour.

A county final for The Nire was a big day and we played well, and we were a good bit better than Ballyduff Lower that day.

We lost the 1987 senior final to Stradbally. We didn't have enough scoring power to beat them. We always found it hard to play against Stradbally. Alo Curran was marking me. He was a tough customer; he was so quick and out first to every ball.

I switched corners at the throw-in but Alo followed me. If I was going to the dugout, Alo was going to follow me!

I missed a lot of 1989. I broke my cheek bone playing seven-a-side soccer and spent a week above in St James' Hospital in Dublin. It was on in Melody's Field. A clash of heads. It drove my cheekbone into my gum. I looked around the ward and I was feeling sorry for myself.

One fella was after getting a belt of an iron bar outside his own door, another fella was involved in a bad accident, another fella got a hiding from someone else. I remember thinking... *My cheek bone is broke... but I'm the best off fella in this ward!*

There was nothing wrong with me!

I couldn't talk and I hate not being able to talk! I was 34 or 35.

That was the first year I didn't start on a regular basis for The Nire. I came on in the drawn county final in 1989 for about three minutes. We were beaten by Kilrossanty, 1-4 to 1-3 in a replay. Imagine only scoring 1-3 in a county final!

That was the day David Kiely gave the famous penalty!

It was no penalty!

The game was in the melting pot, The Nire were a couple of points up and in the dying moments of the game, Kilrossanty got a penalty. Jim Maher buried it and they won by a point. I've been told a lot of different versions. David is a genuine fella; I don't think he deliberately did anything wrong.

I remember walking out of the Fraher Field with Harry Quinn. Harry had the cup and I would have known Harry because I played in a group team with him.

There was a lot of controversy about it. There was a lot of booing going on. Harry just opened the boot of the car and threw in the cup. I suppose it wasn't the best way to win a county final and they haven't won it since.

Paddy Phelan organised a protest outside the Fraher Field the following week. It was before a National League game between Waterford and Clare. I arrived in to see the match because we had four or five fellas playing.

I saw this protest outside. Banners, placards... the full works.

There was a big one in the middle.

FREE THE NIRE FIFTEEN

I was very annoyed over it.

I remember meeting Paddy in Melody's that night and we had a pretty serious debate about it.

'Paddy I was completely against it... we didn't need to do that.'

'If we didn't do it, the same thing would happen next year!' he said.

It reminded me of Margaret Thatcher, the lady who was not for turning. Paddy was not for turning!

I played again the following year. We were beaten by Kilrossanty in a quarter-final in Fraher Field. That was my last game of senior football. I played a bit of junior after that but very little. Waterford were up and running in the ladies football by then so there was no time left to do anything else.

I DID THE video commentary the day The Nire won their first senior title in 1993.

I'll never forget it. They did serious training. Séan Guiry took over as manager but even before that, in my last year or two playing, Ger O'Leary came in from Macroom and Jesus 'twas savage training. *Savage training.*

It was a wet day in Cappoquin. I remember being in the dressing-room after the match and the lads were drowned.

Someone asked me was I disappointed I wasn't playing. My time was gone. I had no interest in a medal, I got as much pleasure out of that county final as the fellas playing in it and I had nothing to do with it. I didn't feel that I missed out. I had been on teams that weren't good enough.

Back in the 80s, when things weren't going well, we might have had seven or eight at training. We had a few fellas like Gerry Coffey, who was great to train but for a lot of other fellas it didn't mean enough.

The Nire management made a lovely touch, they invited the group back to the Keereen Bar out the road to Clashmore, a nice, quiet pub for an hour. They all went back there. It was a really good idea. It was a time for the players to have a drink and then it was back to the Park Hotel for a meal, and onto Ballymac and the Nire school… and everything else that went with it. Magical times!

People tell me The Nire have lost eight county finals but my answer is The Nire have won nine. Nine county titles is fair going in 25 years, and to get to three Munster club finals as well.

The first one against Dr Crokes, that was an opportunity. The day against Austin Stacks, we were in a great position until they had a man sent off. As often happens, when you have an extra man the other team throw caution to the wind. We missed a few chances and gave away two bad goals.

To win either of those would have been the icing on the cake.

The Nire didn't play Munster club in 1993. The county final wasn't finished on time. In 1994, we played Castlehaven. I did the commentary that day with Cork local radio. Paudie Palmer was there as well. They had one from each side. The Nire played well that day. They were special days going away from home playing Munster club games. Larry Tompkins and Niall Cahalane were on that Castlehaven team.

The club has come a hell of a long way. I would have seen what it meant to the likes of Liam Ryan and Billy Grant to win a county junior hurling final in 1963. There were a lot of lean years. I remember being at the 1967 county final, with the Foot and Mouth it wasn't played 'til 1968. Junior football!

From Mecca's Inch, where The Nire started off, to Fenton's Field… to the Millfield… to the Fraher Field and to Munster finals in Páirc Uí Chaoimh.

The club has come a hell of a long way.

WHEN WE WERE young fellas, there always seemed to be a divide and a rivalry between The Nire and Fourmilewater. They were two different parishes.

People on either side would have felt that there should have been more Nire fellas on the team, or more Fourmilewater fellas on the team. Some of the older people would have felt that. As players, it never really bothered us.

For years, it hasn't existed.

The only big regret with the GAA in Ballymac was when they bought the Millfield, with the volume of players that we have now, that the whole field wasn't bought and turned into a community field. That didn't happen. In fairness, they paid £7,000 for the field and that was a lot of money.

To go down to the Millfield any night and see over a hundred young players, four or five training sessions going on and people restricted to a small corner. Someone said to me one time… 'That's shocking', but it isn't really shocking.

What is shocking is clubs with two or three pitches and no one inside in them. That's what I call shocking!

« CHAPTER 12 »

'HEY YOUNG FELLA, I've one for you this morning.'

The postman, Danny Connolly would be into our house every morning before we went to secondary school. He'd be waiting for the door to open at half seven.

He'd come in and have a question or maybe two questions. I liked general knowledge anyway so we'd be answering away bits of questions. Then, there was a quiz in the hall.

I think the hurling club ran it as a fundraiser; my uncle Kieran was the question master. I went down to it and I liked it.

That's where I met John 'Jackson' Kiely.

It was an individual competition. We were all up on the stage together. When your name was called, you walked out to the microphone and answered a question.

It got down to the last three or four and then you had a Grand Final. 'Jackson' Kiely was there and Kiely would prompt everybody! He was larger than life.

Danny Connolly was there, Jim Ryan was very good and Paddy Phelan was a great quiz man as well. It was something I always liked doing. I got involved in question time in Scór when I was about 15 or 16.

One night, my uncle Kieran was asking questions. This young fella came out, probably about 15 years of age, and he couldn't reach the microphone. He had to go up on his tippy toes!

Kieran asked the question, 'Where was John F Kennedy shot?'

The young fella thought about it for a minute.

'In the head!'

The whole place was in a howl!

'Sorry young man... no marks.'

Ah Jesus I'll never forget it!

Kieran was often asked to make out the questions but they were savage. Unless you took part in quizzes yourself, you wouldn't know the difference between a hard question and an easy question. I believe that the question master's role is not to show what he knows himself but to see what the audience knows. If some fella doesn't answer six out of eight, he's going to lose interest. Kieran used to ask savage questions.

Then the pub quizzes started in the late 70s. All the pubs had a team. Jim Ryan, myself, Catherine Murphy, John Kiely and Richard Power represented Doocey's. We started to take it seriously. Gerry Chawke's pub would have been our big rivals.

We used to train for quizzes three or four nights a week. We went into John Kiely's house in Dungarvan and we would go through maybe 4,000 questions. A book each. People used to come in with us who weren't taking part at all. In a night, from eight o'clock until three in the morning, we could go through 4,000 questions, imagine! Rapid fire.

Quizzes were a big deal in those days.

Kiely used to be with us but he was always late. We got to a semi-final against Ollie's in New Inn and Kiely was going to the races in Ballinrobe. Pat Grant was working with me so I paid Pat to go with him for the day to get him back in time.

The final was on in Clonmel and the first year we beat Chawke's. It was beamed out to other rooms in Hearns Hotel because you couldn't get a ticket. We went to New Inn for a quiz and we had two 50-seater buses going from Ballymac! It was huge. If we were in Ballymac, the pub would be full. John Coffey, Mary Coffey, Josie Coffey would be in early to get seats. It just took off. We trained for that religiously.

When I think back on it now, it was absolute madness.

We did it for five or six years in the late 70s and early 80s. We had a serious sports quiz team. We won the Clonmel Sports Pub Quiz by so much the second year that they abandoned it! They didn't have it anymore!

I remember one year we had a good run. We won the Clonmel Pub Quiz, the Cahir Pub Quiz, the Dungarvan Pub Quiz and the Youghal Pub Quiz. We won the four of them.

In those days, the world was a little bit naive. If you didn't know the answer, you asked the question master to repeat the question! You'd think about it.

As we were all sitting together, you'd manage the prompt!

You wouldn't say 'London'... you'd say 'Ondon'

We used to prompt one another! We were all up on stage together but after a year that stopped and it went every second person, so that put a stop to it.

Every team was at it.

We won a big trophy. A huge, big trophy. There's a load of them above in the attic.

Then, *Where In The World* came along with Theresa Lowe on RTÉ.

Kiely had a bad habit.

If he knew the answer, he would blurt it out and he mightn't think it through. If he didn't know it, he would say... 'Ah... ahhh... ahhhhhhh'. There was also a buzzer round.

We got Michael Desmond to make a buzzer. We'd ask him a question and Kiely was sitting in front of me. I wasn't in the quiz at all. Jim Ryan was in it.

Kiely would get a question.

If he didn't answer in two seconds, I'd slap him down on the knuckles with a ruler!

It was no good. While you're thinking about that question, you could answer two more. That's the level it was at. They won *Where In The World* in 1990.

He worked with Willie Trihy before that in the mid-70s and that's when I met him first. Every time at a tea break or when he'd be throwing in a barrow of blocks, he'd have a question for you. We were at a quiz one night down in Clonmel Golf Club with Jimmy Magee. Jimmy was very good.

He threw out a question about a race. Kiely named the winner, the second, the third... the trainer, the jockey... and the price of the three horses.

Magee was just gobsmacked!

But then he could miss his own name! He could answer too quick.

He was great craic.

But Jim Ryan was the best I ever saw at quizzes. He is a great friend of mine, always offering support and encouragement. We also coached Michael Gildea and he won *Know Your Sport* in 1990. He was inside in Jim's house or Kiely's house, and the same thing. Jim, myself and Kiely used to come along an odd time and Michael Gildea. Everything was coachable in those days!

Then, we just lost interest. The whole thing died; people stopped going to it. There was only a few years in it and it just petered out.

I started doing question master in the late-80s. My theory was that everyone should get six out of eight. You'll sort it out in the last round or put a hard one in every round. They'll all go home feeling great. Your job is to entertain.

It could take me six or seven nights to sort out the questions. Every now and again I would throw in a question with three answers. That gives the fella who has no clue a chance of getting it, and gives the really brilliant guy a chance of missing it. A few true or false.

PART THREE

Glory Days

« CHAPTER 13 »

FOOTBALL WAS THE be-all and end-all for those Waterford footballers.

Áine Wall took off a plaster of Paris before the Munster final in 1992.

She broke her hand in the league quarter-final against Monaghan above in Portlaoise. We brought her back to Ardkeen Hospital. The x-ray showed that the bone was broken and it was put in a plaster. They told her that they would review it in five weeks.

The Munster final was on five weeks later.

On the Thursday before the match, at home, her mother Mary went into the sitting-room and Áine was inside dissolving the plaster in a bucket of water.

'What are you doing Áine?'

'It's like this Mum… I'm playing that match.'

She took it off.

We beat Kerry 0-8 to 1-1 in Dungarvan. She scored four points out of eight and put on the plaster again the following morning. Incredible.

That's what those girls would do.

IT WAS LAOIS again in the All-Ireland final in 1992.

We nearly got caught. 2-10 to 3-4.

I remember Ann Fitzpatrick getting clobbered just before half-time at the Hill 16 end. She was down. I went into her. Johnny Hayes was refereeing.

I thought she was semi-concussed because she wasn't moving at all. Jesus, I thought she wouldn't get up, now. In those days, you threw a bucket of water on someone!

She got up anyway. Billy Kelly was there.

She got a thump. Ann Fitz was a tough customer, now.

She wobbled up to her feet.

'Someone is going to fucking pay for this!'

That's exactly what she said!

Jesus, we got a great goal at the start of that game. Bernie put a ball in over everyone's head into Áine Wall from about 50 yards out and Áine caught it, turned back into the Canal End and stuck it.

Laois played really well; they were better than the previous year. We were level at half-time having played with the wind.

We won that match in the first 10 minutes of the second-half against the wind. Geraldine O'Ryan flicked down a ball to Áine, and she stuck it. Marie Crotty kicked two great points.

I enjoyed it even more in 1992. I never realised what it meant and it was harder to win. That was a defining moment for us. Nothing compares to your first one but it was more satisfying to win it twice.

A supporter, Micky Wall (Micky the Mason), got out on Croke Park after the match and he was looking at the pitch.

'Wouldn't it be a grand place to leave off a few ewes?'

A sheep farmer from the Nire!

You'd never get tired of the place. Croke Park.

It changed after winning the second one in 1992.

In the early years, it was absolute euphoria. An unbelievable feeling. It was like climbing Everest. But the more we won, the more I forgot about it straight away and instantly I started thinking about next year. It takes over your life to that extent. When the team bus drove from Croke Park back to the hotel, I was thinking about the following year.

The celebrations were great and it was really nice to see the crowds turning out in Dungarvan. It was a big deal for the girls. It was nice that the public acknowledged what the girls did.

Tom Keith and all those organised some fantastic homecomings and they were magical times around the Square in Dungarvan. There was always time to mingle with people and have a chat, even with people you wouldn't even know. Even to this day, I still meet people who talk about the 90s and the great players we had, and the great team we had. And they were a great team.

I'm actually enjoying it more now when I think back on it, and when I hear some of the players being interviewed and how much it meant to them. I wouldn't have been fully aware of what the players' feelings were at the time.

1993 WAS A PROBLEM.

We went off the boil.

We weren't right all year.

I knew it. I sensed it early in the year. We were off the pace.

We didn't go well in the league. Training was slower and more sluggish. We weren't playing well. We used to be hammering teams.

The bite wasn't there. I had to coax players a bit more. We didn't have the panel to drop people. We were always working off 22 or 23 players. The tendency was to try to be loyal to people who played well in the past.

If it came to it, I had to drop them. It was never easy dropping players but at the same time, I had to do it.

It wasn't a part of the job I enjoyed. I'd always tell them individually first. The players deserve to know that. I'd always tell them at the end of training before the team is announced. If you told them before, it would interfere with training. Privately always.

I still do to this day. Particularly if a player is any way established. Your first line is invariably… 'There's no easy way to tell you this…'

It isn't as hard now because everybody realises that very often the players coming on are the players that are going to win the match. The game has changed but it's still not easy.

It was never for doing something wrong, missing training or somebody acting the maggot… it was always genuine.

We wouldn't have had that many big calls to make but there were occasions that I had to leave people out. We were lucky enough over the years, we never picked up too many injuries. Claire Ryan had a cruciate one year but nothing massive.

I WAS WORRIED in 1993.

We tried to address it but it was very hard to address. People seemed to think that everything would come right on the big day but that's not the way it works.

We played Kerry in Killarney in the Munster final. We struggled all day. Then, Fiona Crotty got a goal to level it with two minutes to go. I felt we had got out of jail and got a replay. We won the kickout again and the momentum was with us.

I think Fiona was blocked down. They went up the other end and Marina Barry got a point to win it. 3-9 to 2-11. They went on and won the All Ireland.

They played very well, now. They had picked up one or two new players. Kerry were still Kerry and it was in Killarney. They didn't like losing three Munster finals in-a-row to Waterford. That was the last time they beat us for 15 years.

We gave them a few hammerings after that.

A lot of our players had been on the go since 1987. An awful lot of football. Going all year round. Some of them were almost coming to the end, like. We got one last kick out of some of them and a few young players started coming through... Rebecca Hallahan, Annalisa Crotty, Julie Ann Torpey, Claire Ryan and Olivia Condon.

I wouldn't say I was shocked by that defeat but I still found it hard to believe. When you're All-Ireland champions for a couple of years and it's taken away from you, it's a tough feeling. It takes a bit of getting used to.

I felt shattered, I felt disappointed. I wondered if I could have done anything else. I played the game over and over. The games I remember as a manager are the games I lost. They're indelibly printed in my mind. Especially the big games.

Winning is great but the ones you lose are the ones that really hurt. And they have to hurt because if they don't hurt, you don't come back.

KERRY HAD A few players who gave it up in 1994. We were out to put down a marker that day.

We hammered them. 1-16 to 2-2. We were miles ahead.

Then, we played Laois in the All-Ireland semi-final in Fraher Field. We won by a point. 1-14 to 3-7. A cracker.

So now we're going into a final having hammered Kerry, getting a real test against Laois and playing a team that had come up from junior two years before that. Monaghan.

We were red hot favourites.

Red hot. It was coming from everywhere. It seeps into players' minds.

Jesus, we got some fright in the final.

That was some game of football.

Monaghan had Brenda McAnespie at full-forward. She scored four points and caused us real problems. They had some lightning fast forwards.

Again, the old trusted two, Áine and Caitriona got the goals. Martina O'Ryan won a ball and came thundering up the field. She laid it off to Áine, and Áine into Casey. That was a great goal. They were goal scorers and so too was Geraldine O'Ryan. Those three players were always capable of getting goals.

Monaghan didn't read the script. They came tearing into it.

They were a tough team. We had a savage rivalry with them. We only became friends with them later on. No love lost there! They were tough cookies and they had a great attitude, they wouldn't be lying down in front of you.

They weren't overawed.

They were physical in a good way. I wouldn't say they were dirty. They were hard. They would plough into you. The speed they started that game at.

We were lucky to get out of that one.

Four points.

2-10 to 0-12.

ANNALISA CROTTY saved a penalty in her first year in goal. She was only 16.

There was underage training in Ballymac and I was a bit late coming back after a match. I arrived into the Millfield and I saw this young one diving across the goals. They were taking penalties on her. I watched her.

Jesus, she was stopping everything.

Patricia Butler was coming to the end. I went over and I spoke to Annalisa. We put her in goal for shooting practice and she was stopping everything.

'Did you ever play in goal before?'

'No,' she said.

'You're playing in goal next Sunday.'

That was it.

In the All-Ireland final, she was the difference. She made three great saves, one of them was that penalty.

We were never afraid to throw on young ones. Annalisa only 16, Rebecca Hallahan, who was on the team the year before at the age of 15, was out with a broken leg. Fiona Crotty was only 15.

Annalisa took to it straight away. She played in goal for four years and then she wanted to come out the field. That was understandable. She had a habit of when she got the ball in goal she would carry the ball out 20 yards and start an attack. That was unheard of.

We did shooting practice once or twice a week and it would be competitive. It would reach a stage where if you missed, you were out over on the other side watching. We played the shooting practice out to the very end until we had a winner.

Everything we did, we tried to have a winner.

Often, we gave push-ups to the girls that lost, just a bit of fun. Five push-ups. Same in the seven-a-side games we had. If you lost, you might have to do 20 push-ups. Everything was geared around being competitive, creating the desire to win and hating to lose.

I remember reading an article about the Kilkenny hurlers. One of them said, 'It wasn't the love of winning, it was the fear of losing'.

I wouldn't say we were at that stage but we weren't far away from it.

« CHAPTER 14 »

WE WERE HOPPING in 1995.

When we went back training, we had a different attitude. We stepped it up to five nights a week.

Brother Lennon started doing circuit training with us in the Friary College in Dungarvan. We were training in the Friary anyway and somebody told me about Brother Lennon, and I went in and had a chat with him.

We hadn't done circuit training before. It was probably the predecessor of gym training. There would be a few bars thrown in and a few weights. It was the 1995 phase of strength and conditioning. He was a no-nonsense man.

He didn't stand on ceremony. No bullshit. Straight up. Stern but at the same time he had the ability to praise or give out. Whatever needed to be done. It also took a bit of emphasis off me because I'd been training the team for years. It was something different.

A new voice, a new face, new ideas.

We were hopping.

We went the entire year unbeaten.

We won the league, the Munster and the All-Ireland.

Training used to be hard. They didn't spare one another. If you played corner-forward on Regina Byrnes or Ann Dunford, you'd know all about it. Martina

O'Ryan moved to midfield and had a great year, and Noirin Walsh proved to be a great captain.

We had 92 sessions that year, 75 training sessions and 17 matches.

We were at our peak.

Everybody was at training early. Five nights a week… and times we trained Friday, Saturday and Sunday. While we were doing that, the Dublin-based girls were training away on their own with Biddy Butler.

Biddy was doing that all through the 90s. Noirin Walsh, Geraldine O'Ryan, Marie Crotty, Caitriona Casey, Patricia Butler and Lorena Mooney would have all been in Dublin. Biddy would have organised that along with Marie Crotty. Marie got involved when she couldn't play herself.

They had no place to train so they used to go out to the Phoenix Park, with deer in the background, find a place where there was nobody else and kick the ball around. They got different venues and different places, literally just where they could find a green, level area.

Early in the year, they didn't come back for training midweek.

The roads weren't as good, there were no motorways. It was a different scenario. Money was scarce. There was no such thing as expenses for ladies footballers, we were working off a shoestring budget. Once it got really serious in the summer, they came back down midweek.

We beat Mayo in the All-Ireland semi-final above in Castlebar. The night that Steve Collins fought Chris Eubank.

Collins wasn't very popular and we took a vote going up on the bus. Who was for Collins, and who was for Eubank? Half of them were for Collins and the other half weren't. You couldn't be listening to him!

There was a press day ahead of the All-Ireland.

I stopped outside Drohan's shop in Clonmel. I had a Toyota Camry. 109AKI. Something happened and it wouldn't start.

I went into the shop.

'I'm in trouble… my car won't start. I'm going up to Croke Park for the press day with the ladies football.'

Jacinta Drohan turned around and took a key off the wall.

'Take my car.'

She just gave me the keys of the car and off I went.

I drove to Croke Park!

Imagine that!

I brought three players up to get used to Croke Park. No bother getting onto the field. In those days, getting into Croke Park was easy enough. We snuck in a football and had a few shots!

I wanted to get the girls used to the place. We did things like that.

You wouldn't get away with it today, would you?

The build-up to 1995 was incredible. Monaghan had won the junior in 1992 and they had put us to the pin of our collar in 1994.

The county really started to get behind us. The support had trebled. Around the county, people were very aware of Waterford now. Whereas in 1986, a few people went. It was building the whole time. More supporters and more publicity.

We were on fire that day.

We won the toss, we played with the wind and it was over at half-time. We were first to the ball, kicked great scores; buzzing, bursting into tackles.

Geraldine O'Ryan was outstanding that day. She caught everything and set everything up. She was key to our team. She played centre-forward and she would bring every other player into the game. She had that ability.

Geraldine was great to win a high ball. She could take on somebody, draw somebody and lay it off then. Or score herself.

We were unbeatable that day. We'd have beaten most teams that had ever played. 4-14 to 1-5.

Eighteen points. The biggest ever winning margin in a final.

That was the day it all came together. I was sad leaving Croke Park that day because I knew we'd never hit that peak again. Every single thing we did that day was perfection.

I couldn't see us reaching that level again and we didn't reach that level again.

That's the trouble with this whole thing, it consumes you.

I'd be on the bus leaving Croke Park and I'd start thinking about next year. That's what it did to me anyway.

You couldn't really celebrate it because you were thinking about next year again. I always enjoyed it but I couldn't stop thinking ahead. Brigid Grant was the same.

Now we'd won four out of five.

WE WERE EVERYBODY'S favourites when we were losing Munster finals. When we started winning and winning regularly at club and county level, suddenly we weren't as popular.

It appeared to us that little obstacles were put in our way. Maybe that's my imagination. As regards fixtures and referees, we certainly weren't granted any favouritism that's for sure!

I'm sure Kerry went through that, and Mayo went through that and Cork went through that. Everybody goes through that when you're on top.

In 1994, Mary Walsh died suddenly.

Mary played for the Waterford minors the week before against Tipperary. Mary was a member of our panel and a lot of our players were minors so they were very upset. For a girl of 18 to die so tragically and so suddenly.

We were playing Mayo in the league semi-final later that week. We asked for a postponement and we didn't get it. We refused to travel and they threw us out. It was inhumane really.

That shouldn't have happened.

Nobody in Waterford was disappointed when Monaghan beat Mayo in the league final! Mayo could have played that game the following week. We were very disappointed over that.

In 2000, we beat Tyrone in the All-Ireland minor final, 7-12 to 1-6, but we brought on six subs. Central Council awarded the game to Tyrone.

My mother was very ill at the time. I got a call from the hospital and I was on the phone for a few minutes. As a manager, you must still take responsibility.

The game was well over. We said at half-time that the senior final is coming up, we won't risk anyone, we'll take off our best players, this game is over. There were five taken off in the second-half but there was one taken off in the first-half with an injury.

After the game, someone said that we put on six subs.

I copped it before the game was over. We were hoping that nothing would happen. The cup was presented. There were a few murmurs about it.

The following morning, I brought in the cup to Dalton's in Dungarvan and got it engraved! They couldn't take off that!

What happened was we both got the same set of medals. We both got winners' medals. The rule was changed after that.

The Tyrone manager Séan O'Kane came down and presented the medals to our team!

THE NEXT TIME, I saw there was something wrong was 1996. I knew it all year.

Monaghan beat us in Aghabog.

The semi-finals were played home and away.

We were off the pace. We had a lot of players that had four All-Irelands won and for some reason, it didn't seem to mean as much. Like 1993, we struggled all year long. We didn't seem to have the zip. I noticed that people were coming a bit late to training and one or two people missed training for what I would consider flimsy excuses.

I had a favourite line one time. Someone rang me up about training and it was raining. So, I told the girls, 'You'll always know when we're training, if you look out and the sky is down on the ground… we're not training. If the sky is not down on the ground… we're training.'

We never cancelled training for anything.

We trained in all kinds of weather. People were missing, they were coming late. You'd know in the sprints, they should drive them a bit harder, they were tailing off. The games weren't as competitive. It didn't seem to mean as much.

We went up the night before. I remember on the bus going up to Monaghan, I felt we were a long way away.

I'll never forget the warm-up. We warmed up near the dressing-rooms and they warmed up at the far end. When they were coming back, they ran straight through the middle of us - a great idea; I'd have been proud of that move myself.

They made a statement in that warm-up.

We don't give a shite about ye.

They hammered us, no point saying otherwise. They were better all over the pitch. They turned an 18-point defeat into a nine-point win. 2-14 to 1-8.

They were miles ahead of us, and they beat Laois in the final. I wouldn't be making excuses about the pitch but it certainly wasn't Clones. It was a club pitch. It didn't win or lose the match. What won the match was they were better.

Monaghan had six players booked. They clobbered us.

« CHAPTER 15 »

'CURIOUS' WAS THE only word Waterford coach, Michael Ryan was prepared to use to describe the decision by referee, Finbarr O'Driscoll to play 11 minutes, 52 seconds of injury time at the end of yesterday's All-Ireland women's football final at Croke Park.

In an extraordinary climax to a thrilling game, Monaghan equalised six minutes into injury time, before adding two more points, in the next six, to retain the title they won for the first time last year. Distraught Waterford players, who had staged a remarkable comeback from nine points down at half-time, to lead Monaghan by a point after the regulation 60 minutes, were at a loss to understand why O'Driscoll had played so much added time after a half of relatively few stoppages.

– Mary Hannigan, The Irish Times, October 13, 1997

THE TOUGHEST DEFEAT to accept.

The toughest of all.

THE LONG COUNT.

We never lost a final until that day. We'd been in five finals, senior and junior, and won them all. We got ourselves into a winning position. With 60 minutes played, we were two points up. With 62 minutes played, we were still two points up. They got a point in the 63rd, and another one in the 65th.

I remember thinking when they got the first point... *This referee is going to play all day.*

A fella called Finbarr O'Driscoll from Cork, living in Dublin. I wouldn't have been best buddies with him. I always felt that he wasn't Waterford's biggest fan.

I met him there lately and I said it to him.

'I saw a TV interview you did and you're still trying to justify the 11 minutes and 52 seconds.'

'I've no problem with that', he said.

That saw the introduction of the clock. There was no issue with time in ladies football before that.

The Sunday Game justified it as well. Pat Spillane justified it. They physically stopped it. Was that ever done before? A draw probably would have been a fair result.

There were injuries during the injury time, some of them were cramp, but it takes a lot of injuries to make up 11 minutes and 52 seconds. Apart from that, I felt the 50-50 calls continuously went against us.

Monaghan were still a good team.

I thought we had it now. We played really well.

The referee can say he gave us chances as well.

'Curious' was the word I used when I was interviewed.

I was conscious about criticising the referee because you'd be suspended. You'd be up before the board. I don't think I ever had many words with referees since I got suspended after the Munster club final in 1984.

It was the toughest defeat to accept. The toughest of all.

The players were devastated. *Devastated.*

Look, referees make mistakes, managers make mistakes... everybody makes mistakes.

There was so much of a furore about it, everybody was giving out. Somebody asked the question is there a better way and should the time keeping be taken out of the hands of the referee. In fairness to Helen O'Rourke and Co, they came up with the clock.

I was delighted to see it. The GAA should have a clock for all games.

Rugby has a clock, American football has a clock, it's a no brainer. Imagine being a referee and the pressure he or she's under.

Definitely, that was the cause of the clock. I remember meeting him after it, the referee. He said to me that he felt he got it right.

'If you got it so right, how come they took the timing away from the referees?'

THE HUNGER WAS back in 1997.

People were enquiring when was training starting. There was a bit of a buzz. A couple of new players came through because we had good minor and under-16 teams. Even if they weren't making the team, they improved training.

We knew it would come down to us and Monaghan. The two best teams in the country. Laois had lost again in the 1996 final so it was hard to see them coming back. We knew we couldn't meet until the final.

We got back on the horse again. Annalisa Crotty saved a penalty in the Munster final against Clare. There was a sea of water on the pitch in Ennis. The game shouldn't have been played.

We got to the All-Ireland final. The first thing I noticed about it; the crowd was much bigger. Monaghan had huge support. *Huge.*

That was a cracking game. Niamh Kindlon got a goal into the Canal End about 20 yards out. A bullet into the top corner. Unstoppable. The best goal I've ever seen in ladies football. And I've seen some good goals.

I wasn't happy with some of the decisions.

Right or wrong, that's what I felt.

We got ourselves into a winning position.

Monaghan fans invaded the pitch during injury time. We got a goal chance near the end. One of our players was through one-on-one with the keeper and didn't finish it.

That was tough to get over.

I remember at the banquet that night, and I'll never forget this… walking over and shaking hands with Jenny Greenan.

'Well done Jenny' I said 'but remember one thing… we'll be back'.

'Don't I know it,' she said.

The two teams were together. That's the way it was in those days. It was crazy because you had one team deliriously happy and the other…

If you lose an All-Ireland, you don't want to dress up and go for a meal. Most people wouldn't take off their tracksuits, they'd be slumped.

We got our first team holiday in January 1998 after losing the All-Ireland. Waterford supporters felt so strongly about that, they did fundraising for a holiday and the money was raised in a week. George Young, Eleanor Hickey and Noel Murray organised a trip to Gran Canaria.

We had three trips; we also went to Tenerife. The whole thing was ahead of its time.

THAT WHOLE EPISODE was the winning of the 1998 final for us.

Initially, we spent a little bit of time feeling sorry for ourselves. There was a lot of anger in the camp because the players weren't happy with the refereeing.

We came back early that year, just after New Year's Day. We had a team meeting every two or three weeks. We involved the players more in it. We knew we had to do something different. We hadn't won the All-Ireland since 1995… it was now 1998. We also knew that some of the players had a good few miles on the clock.

We sat down and we had a chat in the dressing-room after training to see how we were going and reviewed the whole thing. They were self-critical of themselves. They were hard on themselves. If something wasn't right about the performance, they wouldn't be afraid to call it out.

We continuously said that year… 'We're going to win the All-Ireland'.

It was like 1995, everybody was at training, people were there before time. There was no messing around. We wondered ourselves could we do this again because they'd beaten us in two All-Ireland finals and a league final replay. They were on a good run against us. We decided that we'd start again, review the whole thing and involve the players more in the process.

The place was buzzing again, people were training hard, tearing into one another; working really hard and you could sense straight away that the appetite and the hunger was back. They felt hurt. They knew the last two years they hadn't been at their best. They wanted to win this back.

The 11 minutes and 52 seconds was in the back of their minds as well. The rivalry with Monaghan was really cranking up. Monaghan were a crowd that didn't stand back from Waterford, they just tore into Waterford. People were asking.

'Is this team finished?'

'Is this the end?'

Players and management felt like they had a point to prove. This team was on a mission.

Mary O'Donnell came on the scene. She developed into a serious player. She was really talented. She won four under-16 All-Irelands. Brigid Grant was managing the under-16 teams and I would have been going to the games anyway.

She stood out like a beacon.

She was a tall girl and she was a really good footballer, with a great football brain. We started playing her midfield and centre-forward because she could make things happen. She was used to playing with boys teams in Ardmore. She was a big find.

At the end of the championship in 1997, Annalisa Crotty said she was tired of playing in goal. She had been an outfield player all her life. She spent four seasons in goal so she was anxious to come out. You'd know from listening to her that she wanted to do something different. We also knew how good a footballer she was out the field. We needed more mobility and more bite.

She could play anywhere. She was a brilliant marker. She could take the ball out of the backs, set up attacks, cut it off. She was the best girl I ever saw to block down, a full-length dive down on the ball. Fearless.

Then, we had to solve the problem with the goalkeeper. We put another outfield player back into goal, Sarah Hickey. She played wing back in 1997. We had to cajole and coax her into goal. We put her in for bits of training sessions and gradually built it up. It was a straight switch more or less between herself and Annalisa. She was a good shot stopper.

Marie Crotty came on board as part of the backroom team. Her playing career was over with a knee injury. She had a great way with players and she was a good leader. She wouldn't be afraid to tell somebody where they were going wrong either. She called it as it needed to be called.

WE WERE WOUND UP for 1998.

We beat Clare in Dungarvan, 4-11 to 3-7 in the Munster final. One of the Clare players said to me in Lawlors Hotel after the match, 'Ye're not very well dressed but by Jesus ye have some team!'

'I prefer the second one any day of the week,' I said. 'It isn't a fashion show.'

We'd be well dressed coming up to finals but before that, it wouldn't be a big deal.

WE STEPPED UP the physical end of it.

We felt in 1997 that Monaghan had bullied us a little bit so we got in Brother Lennon to give us a hand in 1998.

We had to do something different. We decided that there was no one going to push us around the field anymore. Brother Lennon toughened us up. Training was a lot more physical. More endurance work. Strength and conditioning would probably be the wrong term but a bit more work with weights and a lot of circuit work. He improved the stamina because Monaghan could run. They were fit, they were strong and they could run.

They had probably taken over from us in 1996 and '97. There was no-holds-barred in training. There was nothing soft about it. This was a championship we needed to win.

« CHAPTER 16 »

We have laid that loss to rest now. It is the greatest day of my sporting life.
— Michael Ryan, *Waterford News & Star*, October 30, 1998

NO TWO COUNTIES have done as much for the promotion of ladies football than Waterford and Monaghan.

They made the whole world aware of the great product ladies football was as regards quality, skill, fitness, intensity. It was like two warring tribes. Neither team ever went beyond the bounds of a good, fair, hard tussle. There was no filth.

I'm surprised RTÉ haven't shown back those All-Irelands, they were two massive games of football. We were serious, serious rivals and there was no love lost.

When Monaghan came on the scene, the noise levels went up! They were the first county to bring massive support to Croke Park. Monaghan came out on the pitch with an energy. They burst onto the pitch.

You had two counties whose ladies were giving the success-starved GAA supporters an opportunity to go to the Mecca of Croke Park and they responded. There was a record crowd. 16,421.

The drawn game was on October 4. I remember thinking that Waterford won an All-Ireland on that date in 1959. We were looking for omens! We were looking for anything that might help!

It wasn't looking good at half time. 3-4 to 0-7 down.

Monaghan went for the jugular and they had a serious goal threat all over their team. They caught us unawares.

We were six points down. We gave them a serious rollicking at half-time. I tore into them.

'Do we want the 1995 feeling back again… or come back into the dressing-room as we were last year?'

The good news was we still had 30 minutes to do something about it. We rolled up the sleeves at half-time. Rebecca Hallahan got a crucial goal. The only goal we got. That was the most important score of the two days. That brought us back into the game. Any self-doubts, that got rid of them.

We switched off then. The ball came back off the bar and Ciara McGuinness got a goal. We were caught ball watching.

1-16 to 4-7.

Even though we were disappointed to draw, we felt that we could win this.

It was a victory for ladies football. The ladies game was miles ahead of the men's game and still is if you ask me.

Those three games, 1997 and the two games in '98, made the sport. No doubt about it, they made the sport. The fitness levels, the scores, the free taking, the intensity, the pace. Incredible!

It's hard to believe Monaghan only won two All-Irelands. They should have won more.

The first thing we were afraid of was when will the replay be? We needed three weeks and we got three weeks. We needed every minute of those three weeks.

Annalisa Crotty injured her ankle and missed the drawn game. It was almost daily treatment for the next three weeks to get it right. She was in a bad state. In fairness, Billy Kelly worked miracles.

Annalisa's ankle ligaments were national news! Bits on the radio, bits and pieces everywhere.

'How is Annalisa Crotty?'

She was a household name. She had three All Stars at the time. She went on to win seven. Once she was fit, we felt that we were going to win the match.

We had a meeting the following Tuesday night inside the Friary College and Brother Lennon was there. We all spoke about the next time.

We weren't going to be pushed around.

Our players weren't found wanting. We were much more aggressive in the replay. I wouldn't say we were dirty but we hit hard.

Noirin Walsh and Siobhán O'Ryan met one of the Monaghan players and they hit her so hard, they actually lifted her off the ground and blew her out over the sideline. Áine Wall turned another girl 360 degrees with a belt of a shoulder.

We played on the edge that day.

Everyone was talking about the four goals we conceded in the drawn game. Everywhere we went. Even at mass on the night before the replay!

'Your defence will have to improve!'

That's what the priest said in his sermon!

A lot of our training in the three weeks was geared towards closing down. Our corner-forward, Claire Ryan was back inside her own 14-yard line at times. She was good at that. Claire was a very intelligent footballer. She was good to find the ball. She always managed to be where the ball was. When we had the ball, we all attacked together and we all funnelled back when they had the ball.

Annalisa Crotty was a sweeper. And no apologies for it!

They had a few lethal forwards; Niamh Kindlon, Edel Byrne and Diane Dempsey. Triona Whyte was a very good marker. Siobhán O'Ryan was the best full-back in the country. Noirin Walsh was big and tall. Byrne was very tall, strong and fast. That was the thinking behind putting Noirin back there. Byrne was physically too strong for our smaller players.

We won the toss and Siobhán O'Ryan played with the wind. We always did that. We always backed our fitness. We were a team that could use the ball well. If you're trying to contain a team in the first-half, you use up an awful lot of energy.

Then if you don't start well in the second-half, you're in big trouble. We always played with the wind. Always. Any team I was ever involved with. Get ahead. Make them chase the game.

We knew it was going to come down to one kick of the ball. Funnily enough, the ball went in under the crossbar twice. Twice! Mary O'Donnell in the first-half and Julie Ann Torpey in the second-half.

In the first-half, Mary caused them all sorts of problems. She got that goal from about 40 yards out. She was in a bit from the Hogan Stand and lobbed a ball in high under the Hill 16 goal over Brenda McAnespie.

At half-time, Noirin Walsh told the players to stand up. She was very aggressive actually going around the dressing-room. She was around a while and she was one of our biggest leaders.

Julie Ann Torpey was always capable of breaking up the field. When she got a chance to go, she'd go. We'd reckon she'd get a chance three or four times in a match to attack. She scored that goal even though I don't know if she was going for it! She gave a little dance.

Julie was one of the best players we ever had. She was a really talented footballer. In the early days, Ger Mooney used to bring her up from Kill along with his daughter Lorena to Ballymac for training. Then we moved to the Friary in later years. She was a fantastic footballer. She got Player of the Match in the replay. I'll never forget her interview after it.

'You'll be a hero tomorrow in Waterford,' Marty Morrissey told her.

'Everybody will be a hero in Waterford tomorrow,' she replied.

The most unassuming player. She was one of the first ever attacking wing backs in ladies football. She could play. She could read the game, very skilful and once she had the ball, she very rarely gave it away. A top footballer. The same birthday as myself, August 9!

There were two All-Irelands in 1997 and '98 and it was fair that we won one each. Even though there was fierce rivalry at the time, we became friendly with some of the Monaghan players after it. I'd be good friends with Niamh Kindlon and Brenda McAnespie. Time dims the rivalry. I'd say it was mutual respect.

Sarah Hickey redeemed herself in the replay. She didn't get much cover in the drawn game. Even though we defended much better, they still created goal chances again the second day.

The big debate going into the replay was… could we stop the goals? I think on *The Sunday Game* they tipped Monaghan to win it.

At the end of the day, it was 16 scores to 11 (2-14 to 3-8). That was the difference.

We knew that nobody would beat us kicking points. We had the players to kick the points so if we could tighten up the goals, we knew we could win the match.

Pat Spillane said before the replay that, 'This Waterford team will have no bother kicking points… Ballymac scored 31 points in the Munster club final last week'.

And we did, we scored 1-31 against the Cork champions, Donoughmore.

Pat is always good at doing his research. Sure, he's always throwing out stats. He should be called Pat 'The Stats' Spillane! He's very good at it.

Colm O'Rourke declared that Monaghan would win because of their ability to score goals.

'Colm O'Rourke is wrong,' I told the reporters afterwards.

'Goals don't win games. It was points that won it for us today.'

It was a tongue in cheek remark!

I remember the clock in 1998; we were three points up. It was the last 30 seconds and the ball was down in our attack. A great feeling.

Two neighbours were there for the presentation of the cup. Noel Murray and Siobhán O'Ryan. Living two doors down!

Noel was just finishing his speech and she took the cup! She didn't wait for him to present the cup at all! She grabbed the cup herself!

I still laugh when I think about it!

Noel would be meticulous, now. Noel played a big part in Waterford ladies football. He was Ballymac chairperson, Waterford chairperson and Munster president. He was a great fundraiser and a great organiser.

Deirdre Nagle sang *Dungarvan My Hometown* in the stand.

In the dressing-room afterwards, it was just bedlam. To see people so happy and the noise and the buzz. I remember coming back after doing an interview and Jesus the place was crazy from way outside the dressing-room.

IT WAS THE most satisfying win of all.

1995 was our best performance but we expected to win in '95. We went into the game in 1998 and it was a real 50-50. We were beaten the two previous years by Monaghan and beaten in a league final. For all those reasons. So much at stake, first live television final, the whole country looking on, two great teams and to play really, really well.

It was the greatest day of my sporting life.

In those days, the only lift for Waterford GAA was the Waterford ladies team.

In 1993, we were beaten by Kerry in hurling. I was there. There were years when Waterford won no championship match in hurling or football, in any grade. The ladies were carrying the can for Waterford. And proud to do so. To win that, with so much at stake and all that happened, was very, very, very satisfying!

The newer, bigger and better Brendan Martin Cup lay on the table.

Slowly the dressing-room emptied. I was last to leave as usual.

I made my way down the steps from the dressing-room and up the steps to the pitch. Darkness was descending.

I walked across Croke Park with not a soul to be seen. A glance to my left revealed a giant crane in the North Dublin skyline on the Canal End with a light at the very top. A glance to the right revealed the scoreboard… Waterford 2-14 Monaghan 3-8.

Underneath the new clock stood at 00:00.

I couldn't help the feeling… *This is as good as it gets.*

We kept the blue jerseys after that. White, as I say, is a ghost's colour, like! Blue made us look a bigger, stronger team. Bill Shankly would have used red. White is a pale colour. You look a bigger, stronger, more intimidating team in a full-blooded colour.

Cork always had that theory. We were lucky in it, so for a number of years after that we wore blue. They're gone back to white now.

After that All-Ireland, we were on a high.

After winning such a great game against Monaghan, we had our celebrations and then there was a league game in December.

Laois came to town.

We beat them 15-24 to 1-1 in Ballymac.

Sixty-five points!

That must be a record.

I was with Laois two and half years later, when they won the All-Ireland… despite that 15-24! Imagine that! That's how far Laois came.

We used to try and get a goal in the first minute if we could. The top teams always try and do that. When you're playing against a team that are underdogs, goals kill them. It sows the seed of self-doubt.

We'd be trying to get the ball into Áine Wall early on, and stick one in the back of the net. I never saw a player to get goals like Áine Wall. When it came to finishing, she had the ability to break the back of the net. She scored 7-6 that day.

When it was over, we weren't overly happy. While the game was on, we played it all we could but we didn't take any pride out of beating a team like that. We had young players coming on, they were fighting to get on that team. The regulars knew that there was someone champing at the bit to get on.

Nobody gave us mercy, and I wouldn't want mercy.

I remember the day in Thurles in the Munster hurling final when Cork got 5-31 against Waterford.

Cork had five goals and 30 points got and at the very end, Ray Cummins was clean through and with mercy, he hand passed the ball over the bar. I turned to the Cork fella beside me and said, 'He'll need that goal before the year is out'.

He did. Kilkenny won the final.

Nobody wants pity.

1995 and 1998 were our two peak years. What killed us from there on in was all the football we played at club and county level. We couldn't sustain it, like. We were going all year round. No break.

It was bound to catch up on us and it did.

« CHAPTER 17 »

THE PHYSICALITY THAT day and the physicality the following year, Ladies Gaelic Football weren't happy about it. They felt that the game was getting out of hand.

At national meetings, the top table felt that the game was veering in the wrong direction. People were whinging and moaning.

It was going from 'ladies' football to being very physical. Suddenly, I saw referees going out with a different attitude.

In later years it got physical again because Mayo brought it, Cork brought it and Dublin it.

It's a contact sport!

Waterford and Monaghan were two teams that just ploughed into one another. It was fair game. Nobody whinged, nobody moaned. They were a great side, we were a great side. When you have two fiercely competitive teams, two seasoned teams and they both want to get the ball and they both go 100 miles an hour, there's going to be collisions.

I've never seen a better final than 1998 as regards intensity, the speed of the game, two evenly matched teams, both former winners and live on television. The first final was shown live on *The Sunday Game*. This got the full status. The drawn game was so good that they came back again three weeks later.

Then, the sin bin came in. The sin bin is fine but if there's a doubt, you can't send off someone. The referee has to be certain.

These are big calls, they decide matches.

THE APPETITE WAS good in 1999. We played Monaghan in the 1997 and '98 finals so we couldn't meet in the final in '99. We could meet in the semi-final, which we did.

We travelled up and we stayed in Bray. It was on a Saturday and we went for a walk up Bray Head before the match and we did our team talk up on top of the hill.

There was a bit of a build-up in the papers. Could the two teams repeat the intensity and the fight? It was another ding-dong battle. A real bloodbath above in Parnell Park. No holds barred. No place for the faint hearted.

In 1996 and '97, they had it over us but we had regained the high ground again. With the confidence we got from drawing and beating them in '98, we felt that we were going to win again. And we did.

Geraldine O'Ryan had a magnificent game that day. We used her as a target player up front. We played the ball straight into her and she held it up or scored herself.

I did an interview with RTÉ after the match and the interviewer said to me, 'After winning this... ye'll be hard to be beat in the final'. Sure, we were going to be raging hot favourites against Mayo.

'I'm worried,' I said, 'because we were up at a very high pitch today and it will be hard to get back up to that again'. And we didn't get back up to that again.

We were too wound up that day.

It's a very fine line. Rebecca Hallahan got sent off. It happened in front of the stand. I was a long way away from it but the one thing I remember about it is that there was no big hullabaloo from the Monaghan team to send her off. Nobody roared to the referee. The next thing I saw her getting the red card and what can you do then?

We went to the appeals meeting in Tullamore but we hadn't a chance. I knew going into that meeting, in my heart and soul, that she was definitely going to get suspended. In fairness to the Monaghan management, they submitted a letter before that meeting saying that it was accidental and there was no serious intent. We thought that was worth something but unfortunately it wasn't.

We were hoping that she would only get a month.

She got three.

We were surprised by that because not alone did it rule her out of playing with the county, it ruled her out of the club championship as well. It was a double-edged sword.

She took it badly.

She was absolutely devastated. She was never even cautioned before that in her career.

Rebecca was a big loss. Really fit, carried the ball all day, took on people, set up scores, got scores. She was a livewire. We didn't have that pace in the final and we paid the price.

The players were devastated, absolutely devastated. It would be wrong to say it was like a funeral, but it was absolute *devastation*. We tried to involve her as much as we could but she couldn't be on the sideline and there were so many rules. You almost must be away from the dressing-room. We made her captain the following year.

It reminded me of the 'Tony Keady Affair' in the late-80s when the Galway defender was banned for a year for playing illegally in New York. The Keady thing went on so long that it affected the Galway team and their management for a full year, and it affected us because we didn't know until that meeting who we'd have and who we wouldn't have. We probably got too annoyed over it.

I remember Galway shouting and roaring, and Cyril Farrell lost the head. Our concentration went too. We forgot about what we needed to do and we started feeling sorry for ourselves. We tried to console Rebecca but there's no consolation for missing an All-Ireland final. She previously missed one in 1994 with a broken leg. We tried to turn the attention back to the game but it was always there.

Rebecca was a huge loss but people forgot about how important Caitriona Casey was. She broke her leg in that semi-final. She was a free taker, could get us scores and used the ball well. A huge player for us.

So, we were without two of our players, and Áine Wall went into that final carrying an injury as well. She wasn't anywhere near right going into that final. It was like being without two and a half players but I wouldn't take anything away from Mayo.

DID THEY SURPRISE us? They did a little bit.

We had played Mayo a good few times and we had beaten them a good few times. They had a new management team with John Mullin and Finbar Egan. It would be unfair to Mayo to say we were overconfident.

We heard in the hotel the night before the match that Cora Staunton wouldn't be playing. She was their leading scorer. That didn't help us.

We had prepared for Cora. Of course, we had.

The theory I had about Mayo was that Cora was an individual player. She was an absolute individual. Passing the ball wasn't her greatest strength. She was their best forward. In fact, she was one of the best forwards that ever played the game. I'd say the fact she wasn't there made everyone realise… *The only way we can replace Cora is that everybody else comes up 10 percent.*

The manager came to me before the match and said, 'Cora is injured, we're going to put her on for 30 seconds… will you make sure that nobody touches her'.

I spoke about it in our dressing-room and we agreed that nobody would touch her. They were taking her off after the first play, and they did.

The whole world spoke about Cora coming off, but we didn't have Casey or Rebecca. Rebecca was a driving force on our team, she was a tough woman. Casey would always get a score. Apart from Áine Wall, she was one of our top two scorers from play.

They played fantastic football. The Mayo teams before that seemed to be held back by something. This team brought their A game to Croke Park. It was their first final appearance but they played like a team that were there all their lives. The final score was 0-12 to 0-8.

No question about it they deserved to win that match.

They had a really good midfield pairing. They were physical, they were strong, they played really good football and they ran. Jesus, I remember looking at them and thinking… *This crowd are going to run all day long.* The Heffernans were brilliant footballers; Marcella and Christina.

We had goal chances at the start but we didn't take them. We needed a goal or two. We needed something to create a bit of doubt in Mayo and we didn't do it. Denise Horan was a brilliant goalie. One of the best goalies I ever saw. Tall, good shot stopper. Always seemed to be calm inside in goal. When she got the ball, she used it well.

She made a brilliant save from Áine Wall.

We were flat all day long. Never got going. Second to the ball. They were different to most teams trying to win for the first time. They never panicked. It was just next ball, next ball… next ball.

No complaints, they beat us fair and square. It was the one game in my time that we lost that I would have absolutely no qualms in the wild earthly world about the result.

The best team won.

2000 WAS THE one that got away, no question about it. Even more so than 1997.

Mayo beat us again.

We had 80 training sessions that year. We played really well that day.

Mayo were a bit like us in 1992, they knew how to win at that stage.

We had some newcomers on that team. Angie Walsh, Marion Troy, Brigid Hannigan, Niamh Barry and Mary O'Rourke played in their first final. We had a golden chance to level it but we missed.

Cora scored two goals. I think she took a lot of steps for her first. We put Mary O'Donnell back on Cora. She handled her after that.

That was a great match. A new team. Beaten by a point. 3-6 to 0-14.

Áine Wall had retired. She came back in 2003. Noirin Walsh was out injured. Martina O'Ryan went into the game carrying an injury. Caitriona Casey came off. She hadn't recovered from her broken leg the year before. It took her two years to get over that. At that stage, she had an awful lot of football played.

We should have won the game, we had chances. If we had won that, and with five young players on that team, who knows what would have happened.

'As sure as they are building that new Hogan Stand over there… this team will be back,' I told the reporters afterwards.

I was wrong about that.

« CHAPTER 18 »

I SHOULD HAVE stepped away then.

In 2001, we were missing over half the panel from the previous year.

We knew we were going to be missing a few but one night at training, myself and Brigid sat down and totted up the figures.

Fifteen gone.

FIFTEEN!

Sarah Hickey, Marion Troy, Angie Walsh, Bridget Hannigan, Annalisa Crotty, Mary O'Donnell, Rebecca Hallahan, Claire Ryan, Caitriona Casey, Geraldine O'Ryan, Triona Whyte, Noirin Walsh, Áine Ryan, Julie Cunningham and Ciara Prendergast.

That was some count.

I was numb driving home from training that night.

Six of them went to America, some retired and some had long-term injuries. We had a lot of good young players coming through but you cannot replace 15 players.

You cannot replace five or six players.

It was a devastating blow.

It was the end of that great team.

We didn't think it at the time but it was the end really.

THE FAKE TAN was starting to appear at that stage. When that comes in the door, success goes out the window.

You can't take the fake tan off them! They have it on before they arrive!

I remember Áine Wall saw someone with fake tan lately.

'If we got that in our day… Michael Ryan would make us drink it!'

I always felt that the team was good enough to win another All-Ireland but some of the young players coming through didn't have the same appetite or dedication as the older ones.

The problem was that they had won four under-16 All-Irelands and three minors. They had seven All-Ireland medals and they didn't have the desire and the fight to go on. Too much underage success takes the edge off players.

The world was changing. The standard of living had risen, people were better off, they had more money in their pocket and more money meant more opportunities to travel. The world suddenly became a smaller place.

The J1s came in, America was only a hop away.

Like, where would you rather be, in New York drinking a glass of Bud or running around the Fraher Field? That's serious opposition isn't it?

We had a shadow of a team. We hammered Cork in the first round of the championship but Clare beat us in the Munster final. It was our first Munster championship defeat since 1993. All good things eventually come to an end.

I wouldn't say I was losing my appetite but I was losing my patience a bit.

I got contrary.

I was expecting the player of today to be as good as the player of 10 years ago and that just wasn't possible. They just weren't at that level.

And I hated losing. I used to play my daughter, Michelle in draughts. When she got to 10, I couldn't beat her so I gave up playing because I couldn't bear to be beaten!

I hate losing.

I *hate* losing.

It was the longest spin home after losing. I would be quiet. I would be analysing it. I would be mad at myself.

Why didn't I do something different?

I just took defeat very badly. It wasn't that I couldn't accept it, I was just so disappointed.

When I'd go home after losing a match, my wife might say to me, 'Why are you not talking?'

'I don't want to talk.'

I'd go into my shell and that was it. I didn't want to talk about it. I didn't want to talk at home about it.

I always went out on a Sunday night. Only three or four pints, I wouldn't be falling down the path. I'd probably talk about the match there, but it wouldn't be the best chat in town.

I HELPED LAOIS win their first All-Ireland in 2001.

We had played Laois in a challenge match. Séan 'Goggie' Delaney was in charge of Laois. He was a confident, cocky kind of guy. A big man. Good hurler and a good footballer.

Goggie rang me. I'll never forget it.

'Will you come up and give us a hand?'

This was early on in 2001.

'Are you joking me? I'm the Waterford manager.'

'Come up and give us a hand.'

'Are you codding me? I'm the *Waterford* manager.'

'Ye won't last long... half your team are gone to America, ye'll be out of the championship soon.'

Clare beat us and the following Monday night he rang me.

'Come up and do a session.'

'Go away from me, I don't want to talk about ladies football.'

He rang me again a week later.

'Come up and do a session.'

'Ok so.'

I drove up to Crettyard, Sinéad came with me and I did a good session with them. I was very impressed the first time I saw them. I was driving down from Crettyard... I was gone about five miles and the phone rang.

Delaney again.

'What time are you up Thursday?'

'I told you I'd go up and do one session!'

He stayed 20 minutes on the phone and I ended up going up for two months!

Once a week for six or seven weeks coaching. Somebody else would do the running, I'd take the football.

They got to the All-Ireland semi-final and he asked me to go to the game.

'No I won't,' I said.

'Why not?'

'If Mayo see I'm around, it will only drive them on. Give your phone to somebody who knows nothing about football and I'll watch the game at home on television. If there's anything I need to tell you... I'll ring.'

He gave his phone to the bus driver. I rang him two or three times... only small things. The driver came down and had a word once or twice. When the game was over, they were out on the pitch and this fella came up and shook hands with Goggie and said, 'Goggie, that was the best I ever saw Laois play but why were you talking to the bus driver... he knows nothing about football!'

Then we were getting ready for the final and the TV cameras came down. I pulled in when I saw the cameras.

'I'm not going near the place tonight,' I told Goggie.

'Are you mad?'

I ended up going into a shed! It was dark out and I gave an hour inside the shed in the pitch dark!

We didn't want to let Mayo know that I was involved.

It came to the final. I was going up twice a week at this stage.

I suggested we go to St Vincent's for a kick around because we'd often gone there before.

Goggie was pulling on a cigarette... 'What do you think?' he asked.

'I can't tell you what will happen in the game but right now they're exactly where they need to be.'

They were hopping.

I sat down on the floor in the middle of the bus going to Croke Park.

'What are you at now?'

'Look,' I said, 'keep this quiet.'

When I came off the bus, I walked straight through to the Laois dressing-room and out, and went for a walk around the pitch. Just as the game started, I sat on a bench.

A Mayo mentor was passing.

'What are you doing there?'

'The stand is full!'

Tensions were high in the Laois dressing-room at half-time. Goggie was giving out. Sue Ramsbottom wasn't happy. I remember catching Goggie.

'You sit down there and we'll win this match.'

It came down to the last kick of the game. Cora Staunton caught a kickout inside her own 20-metre line. Mary Kirwan took the free. I was afraid she wouldn't take it in time because there was only 20 seconds left. As the ball was going over the bar, there was about one second left. I was delighted Laois won it because they had lost so many.

Jesus, they went cracked!

Bedlam!

Absolute bedlam!

I enjoyed that one, too! More so for the fact that Laois had suffered so much, rather than the fact of someone beating Mayo. They were going for three in-a-row.

I was up in Laois three times afterwards for funerals. Goggie died, the secretary Mary Ramsbottom died and Lulu Carroll died. Three times in a couple of years I was up at funerals.

You couldn't say no to Goggie, he was larger than life. His language was atrocious! The cursing!

Back in 1994, we played Laois in Dungarvan in the All-Ireland semi-final. We beat them by a point and to be honest about it we got the rub of the green, they weren't happy with one or two refereeing decisions.

It was our third time beating them in four championships. Two finals and a semi-final. On the way back, they stopped for a drink. Up the country somewhere.

They had a good few drinks and one of the players said to Goggie, half-jokingly, 'You're only in it for the money!' Goggie took out the expenses cheque he had and tore it up in front of the girls!

'Now, am I in it for the money?'

The following day, he had to ring Margaret Brennan from the county board to reissue the cheque! That would be Goggie!

Fellas like him make the whole thing worthwhile because you'd be in stitches in their great company!

I WAS HOPING to win another All-Ireland with Waterford.

A lot of those young players had come through with myself and Brigid Grant, and I was hoping that it would happen. In 2002, it should have.

We won one more Munster against Cork and one more league final against Mayo. Michelle was drug tested after that Mayo match. Herself and Deirdre Breathnach. The first time I saw drug testing in ladies football.

We were beaten in the All-Ireland semi-final by Monaghan. The referee didn't help.

Jesus, I was very unhappy that day. Marty Duffy booked three of our players in the first 10 minutes for their first foul. He told them the next foul, they would be sent off. They were afraid to tackle.

I rang Marty after that game. At his own house. I can still hear people talking in the background. It was a week after the match; I knew by then his match report was gone in. He couldn't report me!

I told him how unhappy I was over what happened. I didn't abuse him or anything, but I asked him what was the thinking behind it? How could players be booked for their first tackle? Innocuous tackles.

We agreed to differ! He turned out to be a good referee and refereed a men's All-Ireland football final.

I found in later years that I got less angry with referees. I realised there was no point. He's not going to change his mind. There's a percentage of referees who like to be the centre of attention.

The minute you challenge him, you're giving him the chance to be the centre of attention. I'd often ask players… 'When was the last time you saw a referee change his mind?'

What he will do is, the next 50-50 decision, he'll give it against you. That's human nature.

Some of the team of 2002 were there in 1991, some were there in 1987 and '88. Some miles on the clock.

I stayed on for a couple of years and then I had three girls on the team. When your daughters are playing, you're either too hard or too soft on them. In my case, I was too hard on them so I felt it was time to move away.

Cork came with a really good team in 2004. We played them in the Munster semi-final in the Fraher Field. Only four of the team that played in 2000 started. We brought Mary O'Rourke home from America for that game. That was a mistake.

Mary was a good footballer but that was no preparation for a match. We were beaten by four points. We hit the bottom of the post with a few minutes to go which would have put us level. They beat us for the first time in 19 years in the championship. We used to hammer them for fun.

They celebrated like they won the All-Ireland. Spectators on the pitch, players went crazy. That was a very significant day for them.

That was the changing of the guard.

A couple of years before that, we played Cork in a league game and they couldn't field a team. They gave us a walkover. Eamonn Ryan came on board and he was a fantastic coach.

They started winning at under-14 and under-16. It was inevitable.

At the end of the day, for every human in Waterford, there's five and a half in Cork! If they're organised, they're bound to be good.

I STEPPED AWAY in 2006.

I should have given it up a few years earlier.

My time was gone. I was 25 years in the job. That's almost as long as Nelson Mandela spent in jail!

I toyed with it a couple of years earlier. Brigid told me one year to stay on and somebody else said it another year. People wanted me to stay and then I was hoping that all of those young players would come through. It just didn't happen.

I remember my last game above in Breffni Park. Armagh beat us but I had my mind made up earlier on that year.

I spoke at length in the dressing-room.

I said I had been thinking about this for a good while. I would have told a few people close to me earlier on that year. Brigid would have known, and possibly one or two players, that this was it. It was time for them to do something else and me to do something else.

A lot of players were emotional. A couple of players were in tears. I thanked them for all their dedication. I told them that I felt we could have won another All-Ireland or two. I told them to stick together and who knows what will happen.

They were a young team. I told them that it would be good for them to have a new voice in charge and to be always proud to wear the Waterford jersey. My time had come and gone. I enjoyed every minute of it.

I was just thinking driving away, that Breffni Park was a very famous place over the years. Cavan had won about 40 Ulster titles and I'd often heard about Breffni Park and fellas like Charlie Gallagher and Ray Carolan. It's a lovely stadium. It's like a bowl down under the ground.

I remember thinking… *This isn't a bad place to end it all.*

After starting in Ballyclough! In a farmer's field!

It was a long journey home, I remember it well.

I drove back. I don't know why I drove!

It seemed to take about five hours. A lot goes through your mind.

I reflected on all the good days we had, all the things we won and the things we didn't win.

It was an important part of my life and I was just giving it all up. It's hard to do that. I knew it definitely needed to be done. I was happy with the decision.

Enjoyed every minute of it. The only thing I'd change are a few results!

The biggest disappointment was to win four under-16 All-Irelands and three minors and not get a senior All-Ireland out of it.

I went home, I gave it up. I didn't think I'd be getting a phone call from Pat Grant the following Monday night! He asked me if I was interested in becoming a selector for the Waterford hurlers.

The whole thing began again.

PART FOUR

Dream Job

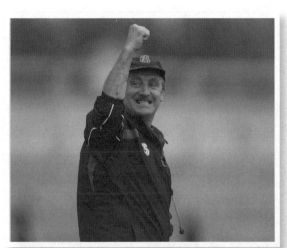

« CHAPTER 19 »

THAT PHONE CALL changed my life.

'Waterford are looking for a new selector… Justin's been told he needs a new selector.

'Are you interested?'

'Let me think about it,' I said.

He rang me back two days later and I said I would be interested. It changed the direction I was going in completely. I was coming from ladies football into the backroom team of one of the best hurling teams in the country.

About 1993 or '94, I would have liked to have a real go at the Waterford hurling job. Hurling was going badly and I had the top ladies football team in the country. It did occur to me around that stage. Tony Mansfield took it in 1996. It occurred to me, but I never took it any further than that until Pat Grant rang me. It was a real surprise phone call.

At training, everything was organised. You didn't have to look for anything. With the ladies football, it was a struggle to make ends meet for years. Suddenly, you were there with two physios, a hundred sliotars and gear almost being thrown at you.

My wife used to say, 'Jesus… you're bringing home more gear!'

I got so many sets of everything.

I looked around the pitch and saw Tony Browne, Paul Flynn… Ken McGrath.

It was on a different planet because they had the resources. The ladies used to get a garda escort for the All-Ireland final; the hurlers got it for a league game in New Ross.

Hotel after a match, the best of food, Gerry Fitzpatrick… a top class guy doing the strength and conditioning, gym programmes, nutrition… everything they needed was there. I wouldn't have seen anything like that before.

I soon adapted.

JUSTIN WAS GREAT craic, very witty. Very serious when he had to be. A lot of people found different faults in him but he was very good for Waterford. Gerald McCarthy had put a system in place as regards discipline and what you needed to do. Justin polished off the whole lot.

He was the missing piece of the jigsaw.

People used to say if Cork beat Waterford, Justin is happy with that. The direct opposite was the truth. Justin would be going through the roof the week we'd be playing Cork. He couldn't beat Cork by enough.

He was dying to beat Cork.

A lot of people have talked about his management skills but everyone has their own way of doing things. He produced a top class team that were very unlucky because at the time Cork were going for three in-a-row, and Kilkenny were the best team of all time.

The only thing that disappointed me was that the panel was picked before my first meeting. We met in the Park Hotel for a selectors meeting. Kevin Ryan was at that meeting but he soon left to take over a club in Wexford. Nicky Cashin, Seamie Hannon and Justin were there as well.

We had a players meeting.

Justin said that there's no point everybody speaking.

'I'll speak and Gerry Fitzpatrick will speak.'

I was determined to speak at that meeting, and I did. The first thing that struck me was that these fellas really wanted to train. They had a great attitude. Very serious about their hurling; drink wasn't an issue and they were really proud to play for Waterford. Above all, nice fellas. No big airs or graces about them.

I would have heard the stories of players from different clubs back in the 1980s and 90s not gelling too well. This was like a club team.

I was the maor foirne. I was the man carrying Justin's instructions out onto the pitch. If something was wrong, I was in and out.

When we were picking the maor foirne, Justin said, 'You better do it… you're the youngest!' I wasn't a young fella at the time!

I felt that I had a say in picking the team, I was happy with that. People said we had no say, but we had a say. If it was two-all about a player, Justin had the casting vote and that's the way it should be.

The first match was down in Wexford in Wexford Park. Kevin Moran was full-forward. We won that game. The whole thing took off then. We beat Kilkenny in the league final in Thurles.

I remember speaking in the Kilkenny dressing-room. First of all, it was so quiet, so respectful, everybody listened and I remember thinking… *They're a quality bunch of players.* They genuinely shook hands, several players on the way out.

'I know ye'll be back,' I said. Sure as God, they were back and came back many times after that.

We had an excellent training camp in Portugal, organised by Justin and Gerry Fitzpatrick. Browns in Vilamoura.

We were like professional athletes for a week. Up every morning at eight o'clock, breakfast, three training sessions a day; one of those in the gym, onto the pitch, lunch, a rest and go back training in the evening when the sun had gone down a bit. Top class facilities.

Justin was all hurling.

Speed of your hurling, speed of your striking… and first touch.

He was massive for building up the players' confidence. He made players believe in themselves. His team talks were very good. People will say they got boring at the end but after six years they were bound to get a bit boring. You can only trot out so much.

His line was… 'We're Waterford. We're as good as anybody or better'.

We shouldn't be paying homage to anybody. He'd say to a guy, 'If you're marking him, don't fucking be standing away from him… show him what you're here for'.

He also improved our hurling immensely. Those were his two biggest strengths.

He had a good way of dealing with players. Maybe people who weren't starting or from 20 to 30, he could have handled that differently. I wouldn't be critical of him.

We were a bit unlucky and we had an awful lot of individuals playing. We had a lot of fellas, despite what you'd do, who would play off the cuff and they were great at it. John Mullane, Eoin Kelly, Paul Flynn and Dan Shanahan were all super hurlers.

Justin believed a certain amount in tactics but it wasn't the biggest thing. Trust your hurling. Believe in yourself.

Trust yourself.

Trust the fella beside you.

There were aspects of a game plan. What's a game plan, like? Dan would come out from full-forward under puckouts or go in full-forward. Seamus Prendergast would come out from full-forward under puckouts.

There were flashes of a game plan. But was it down in black and white on paper? No. Instinct played a huge part in it.

Those players were outstanding individuals and then you had Stephen Molumphy inside in the middle of them and Seamus, two real team players. I often felt that if we put together one or two more passes in games, we'd have been even better.

The year I was there was probably their best ever year.

We played Cork five times that year and beat them four times; in the league, the league semi-final, the Munster Championship and the All-Ireland quarter-final replay in Croke Park. That Cork team were 70 minutes from three in-a-row. Justin revelled in that.

The three games in two weeks in Croke Park killed us. We were wrecked.

I mentioned it to Pat Flynn, the chairman of the county board, before the throw in of the replayed Cork game.

'Waterford and Cork should meet before this ball is thrown in and tell Croke Park whoever wins this game is not going to Croke Park next Sunday.'

We didn't try as a management team to put the game back a week. The two weeks before that going up on the train, fellas were doing puzzles, doing quizzes, shouting around and the craic was mighty. The last week I walked up the train, and half the team were asleep on the way up. They were wrecked.

Limerick hit us with a tornado.

Brian Begley destroyed us. Donie Ryan as well. I did a coaching session with his club after in Garryspillane. Donie arrived in with a pair of wellingtons on! A gas ticket!

They got the goals. Five goals.

Looking back on it now, we were probably a bit complacent having won the league, beaten Kilkenny and beaten Cork twice. They sat back, had a week off and watched us. Waterford always find it hard to beat Limerick. They were a physical team.

I didn't like Richie Bennis' interview after the game.

'We got five goals and Dan The Man got none,' he said.

Dan Shanahan got 8-12 in that championship and four points that day.

Looking back, we should have made a real stand. With the GAA, I don't think it would have made any difference, of course.

Before big matches in Thurles, we used to go into St Patrick's College, a seminary. We were playing Cork and we went for a lazy puck-around in the college.

Come out through a basketball court, and there was a hurling pitch and there was a long building down by the side of it, and there was a two inch downpipe down the wall.

Flynn came out last. The lads were taking pot shots at the downpipe. Flynn comes out hopping the hurley off his heels and sits down in the sun and is watching the lads taking a few shots. He got up.

'Stand back,' he says.

Thirty yards, he hit that downpipe dead on. Thirty yards!

Then we were coming off the pitch, going through the basketball court and he had the ball on his hurley. The backboard is at the other end of the basketball court. He said to Mullane, 'What do you think?'

'Go for it!'

He struck that ball the length of the basketball court, hit the backboard and dropped the ball down into the net.

Then we go to Thurles and the match; Kelly is on the frees unless we're looking for a goal. We thought it would improve Flynn not to be depending on frees. It would bring him more into the game and make him work a bit harder.

We got a 21-yard free out on the wing and Cork dissented. The ball was moved right in front of the goals, so my job was to tell Flynn to take it. He took the free along the ground into the back of the net.

We walked down to Liberty Square after it and Flynn was beside me and I said, 'I've watched dozens of videos of you and they all go in under the crossbar'.

'Watch it again… they're hitting their hurleys off the crossbar.'

He had the presence of mind.

Munster final. It's wet.

Free out towards the sideline. Someone injured. I'd always have a dry ball in my pocket. I said to Flynn, 'Do you want a dry ball?'

He walked over, a Limerick fella had a ball on the sideline and he took the ball!

He wouldn't kill himself training but he was exceptional. He was a rogue, an absolute rogue. Dan was salt of the earth. Kelly was an unbelievable talent. Molumphy was your dream man. Seamus gave it all and got the best out of himself. Flynn was a genius, no point saying anything else. Mullane, five All Stars speaks for itself. I felt if we put one or two more passes together in games, we could have got more goals.

We went to Orlando in January 2008 and the mood was okay.

Justin decided to start back training a little bit later. We had a poorish league campaign and just never got going.

We went on a training camp in Portugal. Again in Browns in Vilamoura. It was nowhere near what we had the year before. For some reason, it just never got going. It's like anything, when you do something for the first time, it's really good.

When you go back and do the same thing again, it doesn't work. That was an indication that we weren't right. When you're going well, those things just don't happen.

Justin asked the players to have a chat amongst themselves which surprised me. If things aren't going great and there's a meeting, you have to be there. He was looking for a report back and they hadn't it finished.

Eventually, they came back with nine or 10 points. There was nothing major in it, change around a few things. They were looking to change up the drills but there was nothing I thought that couldn't be easily solved.

One of the requests was to drop a selector. Seamie Hannon. That was a big one. That really annoyed Justin.

In fairness to Seamie, he was in a difficult situation. He was farming and early in the year, he was finding it hard to get to training. Justin spoke about retiring and stepping down to us as a management team. He was furious, now.

When the camp was over, we went back on the plane and Michael 'Brick' Walsh sat in beside him on the way home for a chat. Brick was a great guy to sort out problems. He was a really good captain as well. We got onto the bus and Justin announced that he was staying on.

It's like everything else, when you're there a long time, cracks start to appear. He brought Waterford a long way and maybe he brought them as far as he could.

Then, we played Kilkenny in a challenge game down in Walsh Park, hurled well and won the game.

We were up against Clare in the Munster Championship at the Gaelic Grounds in Limerick. We were short Ken McGrath, Eoin Kelly, Paul Flynn and Eoin Murphy. Four of our top players. Four All Stars.

Justin decided to go to the Clare side of the city, to a hotel for a warm-up, which surprised me. Nobody questioned him, he was the manager. We were out at the front of the hotel doing a bit of a warm-up. It was more of a puck-around than a warm-up; it was very, very warm.

The Clare crowd were passing blowing the hooters in the cars. I wouldn't read anything into it. If you lose a game, all these things surface. If we had won the game, there'd be nobody talking about that. I didn't think it was anything significant at the time. People said it after. We just met a Clare team that caught fire.

I saw the incident between Justin and Dan. I was the maor foirne, I was close enough to it. I still think that wasn't deliberate from Dan; I just think Dan was disappointed with his own performance. I don't think there was any attempt to snub Justin.

I didn't see it that way anyway. Dan was disappointed to be taken off number one and disappointed with his performance number two.

There was complete silence in the dressing-room after it. In those days, under that system, we wouldn't be playing again for a few weeks.

The players were in having a drink in the hotel and they were slow coming back to the bus. We were on the bus and a number of players were inside. I went in to bring them back out. I didn't rush them, I gave it 15 or 20 minutes and they came out.

I said, 'Lads… the bus is going shortly'. I didn't push them.

I coaxed them to come back out on the bus. There was no big deal about it. Some of them had half a drink and I knew better than to try and force them. It would be the wrong thing to do. Eventually, they came out. Séan Power came in as well.

I knew coming home from Clare that we had a job on our hands. The fact that some of the players didn't travel home on the bus wasn't a good sign anyway.

I didn't think it would turn out the way it turned out. I knew that players weren't happy. They probably weren't happy with the way they played. After all, it should be said some of those players asked Justin to stay on the train home from Dublin the previous year. Dan was one of them.

It was like a team that had been together for six or seven years and hadn't done it. It was a natural thing that happened.

Justin's appetite never went. His appetite for the game will never leave him until the day he dies. I knew things weren't right though. I could sense that the same buzz wasn't at training. The games weren't as well contested.

It looked as if it became a bit of a chore. The bite wasn't in it. I thought it would turn around though. I thought we got a kick up the ass and by the time we got a couple of weeks' training in, it would turn around. I genuinely thought it would turn around.

There are rumblings against every manager, you'll always have people giving out. I thought it could have been sorted out.

Justin rang me on Thursday morning. I remember exactly where I was… building houses in Deerpark. I can still picture the spot when the phone rang. When I saw his number coming up, I didn't think that was the news.

Justin was always a fella that would get straight to the point.

'The players want a change, I'm stepping down.'

The two selectors were stepping down as well. I thought about it for an hour and rang him back and I said I was stepping down as well. We were all in it, we might as well all step away from it.

For a fella that had done so much, it was a tough way to go. He did an awful lot for Waterford hurling. He gave them the belief, the confidence and the swagger. He lifted the whole profile of Waterford hurling. He made them the fashionable team to follow.

He gave them an identity. They played some fantastic hurling along the way and were involved in some of the greatest games ever played.

I rang him once or twice after that.

I remember ringing him about Limerick and I advised him not to go near it. Obviously, he made his own mind up about it. I just said to him, 'If I were you, I wouldn't get involved in that'.

I haven't talked to him since, really. I'm sure he was very hurt over it but he didn't express it to me. He had to be.

DAVY FITZGERALD CAME in.

I remember watching *The Sunday Game* and Davy was auditioning for the job that night, I thought. Davy came in and there was a big buzz like any manager that comes in but particularly Davy. A rising tide lifts all boats.

I remember hearing stories about them training harder and people questioning our fitness that year, and maybe we lacked a bit of fitness because Justin decided to start training later. I could understand why Justin tried it because this was a team that was on the road a long time. His target was the latter stages of the championship, he wasn't too bothered about Munster. He never spoke about that but I got the feeling that his target was the latter stages of the championship.

Unfortunately, he never got a chance to do it. Then Davy came in, and there was all the noise in the world and stories about gear being washed and gear being brought home. That's good because it's something different. The team needed something different.

You'd have mixed emotions. I was still disappointed.

I lost interest for a while. I stopped going to games and there were other things happening. I'd be always hoping that Waterford would win though.

They won the first couple of matches without being impressive. I was at the Offaly and Wexford games in Thurles. There was nothing to suggest they were going to beat Tipp in the semi-final. That was a really good performance. I watched that game on television. They deserved to win it. I remember thinking that they've got a chance in the All-Ireland final.

I would have been talking to Nicky Cashin every now and again.

We were and still are very good friends. I asked Nicky was he going to the final and Nicky didn't want to go, but I said, 'Look... we'll go'.

We went to the final and Jesus it was a horror show. Nicky went away at half-time. He said, 'I'll talk to you tonight'.

Nicky had turned to me before the game and said, 'They're going to get hammered!' He would have been familiar with what was happening in Kilkenny.

Just as the ball was thrown in, I was looking around the field and Waterford fellas were getting involved with Kilkenny fellas, and it didn't add up. Everything just went wrong. I remember Ken failed to lift a free.

All over the pitch, we were losing the battles. That was the wrong day to play Kilkenny. They were at their absolute peak. If Waterford were at their absolute best, Kilkenny would have still won that game by seven or eight points.

They blew us away. It was hard to watch.

I was worried about the build-up because the whole county went crazy. All the papers blowing it up… the radio.

I was wondering could we deal with that. We didn't deal with that.

I was only there for a year and a half. You could argue that the first year was the best year Waterford had since 1959. It was disappointing that it all came to an end so quickly. I felt with a few new players that things would improve and then suddenly you're not involved and you're on the outside.

You drift off to other things. It just happened like that.

« CHAPTER 20 »

EOIN KELLY from Mullinhaone rang me a month after the All-Ireland. It got the fire going again.

I was up in Dublin one day and the phone rang.

'Eoin Kelly here... Mullinahone. We're looking for someone to manage the team. Would you be interested?'

I was in Bewleys having a cup of tea.

'I'll be there in five minutes,' he said.

He called in.

I HAD A really enjoyable year with Mullinahone. We won the South championship. We beat Killenaule in the final after they hammered us early on. I was manager and I had a fella called Séan O'Meara with me.

I had to move on to delegation. By that time, I'd given a year and a bit with Justin. It was more delegation than coaching. I didn't do a lot of coaching.

As a manager, I've learned over the years. For many years I was on my own. I've learned to use a management team.

I wouldn't want 'yes men' in there, I'd want people with a concrete opinion. You listen to everybody and as a manager you have the final say. If there were four selectors and me and the four of them said this and I said no, I'd go with the four.

If it was two-all, I'd go with myself.

I couldn't get over Eoin Kelly's attitude. He was crippled with injury but he would be there at every training session, carrying cones. He'd ring me Monday wondering what I'd want for the week. He was a top, top guy.

He was top notch to talk in the dressing-room. He never said anything that he wasn't prepared to do himself. No ranting or raving. He had the ability to find the right balance between giving out and praising. He was so respected. He treated those South championship games and that South final like an All-Ireland final.

Eoin was incredible and so was Paul Curran. Two great club men. They drove the whole club on. The pride in Mullinahone, that whole club, was incredible. It meant an awful lot to them.

We were beaten in the quarter-final of the Tipperary championship by Upperchurch-Drombane. The game was a draw and they beat us in extra-time. Incredibly, a fella hand passed the ball over the bar and the ref allowed it.

I couldn't believe it. In Semple Stadium?

Mullinahone wanted me to stay another year but Brian 'Bull' Phelan rang from De La Salle. I met Eoin Kelly, Paul Curran and the goalkeeper, Séan Fox in Clonmel.

'Lads, to be honest I want to go back to Waterford.'

Eoin said to me afterwards, 'At this point in time they're the Munster champions, you can't turn that down'.

There was no respect for the South teams in Tipp. It was all about North and Mid Tipp. The assumption was it was all football despite fellas like Babs Keating and Mick Roche. John Leahy was a tremendous hurler. They didn't respect the South teams. That's the way I saw it. They didn't respect them.

For a long time, there might be only two or three South fellas on the panel. Same thing in Waterford. The West teams weren't respected. Tallow, Ballyduff and Lismore changed all that.

There was a lovely homely atmosphere in Mullinahone. Jackie Bolger used to make the tea every night after training. Even though he was training other teams, he'd always be back to make the tea. I never left Mullinahone without a cup of tea, a biscuit and a chat.

I got a phone call at the end of 2008 from the Dublin ladies.

A lady called Kathleen Colreavy rang me and she asked me would I be interested in joining the Dublin management team. Then, the manager Gerry

McGill rang me. I went to the first training session, the day De La Salle won their first Munster club title. I said I'd give them a hand once a week. It ended up being twice a week in the finish. They were beaten in the final by Cork.

Tommy Brown, a Dub, and Mick Browne, a Westmeath man, were selectors. Gerry, Tommy and Mick all taught in the same school in the centre of Dublin. Jim Kilty did the coaching and then they got in Martin Kennedy, who later worked with the Dublin hurlers and footballers. Pablo Gilheaney was a great character, a real Dub.

I did some motivational stuff and gave a few team talks.

The second year they won it, they beat Tyrone but I missed the final. De La Salle were playing on the same day. Waterford were also playing in the intermediate final.

I was there again the following year; they were beaten by Cork in the All-Ireland. There was a very controversial sin bin; Sinéad Goldrick got a yellow card for what I don't know.

Maybe I know nothing about refereeing!

DEREK McGRATH GAVE me analysis on the De La Salle players when I took the job. I met him just inside the door in Lawlors Hotel in Dungarvan.

It was handwritten on A4 size pages.

Analysis on every single one of the players. It was absolutely outstanding. He summed up every player. I remember Dean Twomey and he wrote, 'This is a man waiting to explode'.

It was so good and it was so accurate. Absolutely top notch. It was all so positive. I'll never forget it. It was a huge help to me. It was obvious, even at that stage, that he had a great hurling brain. I'm not surprised that he went on to be a county manager.

De La Salle felt that they had the ingredients but they just needed a new voice or a new face. I had two mentors, Ray Murphy, who did the coaching, and Luke Lawlor. They were two good lads around the team. The players were great to train and the field was always full. If the county team weren't training, Kevin Moran would be in early in the year to do the warm-up; John Mullane was around the place as well as Brian Phelan.

There was a fierce loyalty to the club by the De La Salle county players.

We got a rude awakening when we got hammered by Ballygunner.

Fifteen points.

Absolutely hammered.

How can his happen?

We had a good players' meeting after that.

Nobody was happy.

The club wasn't happy.

The players weren't happy.

I wasn't happy.

We had a really good clear the air meeting. I remember we went out and trained really well after it. In fairness, everybody took responsibility. Players did and management did. We played a few challenges outside the county and the whole thing just took shape. We qualified for the quarter-finals and we played Tallow.

We won every match we played. Everybody bought into it. We didn't start hurling until June or July, so we were very fresh for the rest of the year.

We got to the county final, against Ballygunner. The lads were dying to get out on the pitch. I could sense it in the dressing-room. It was almost a question of having to calm the lads down. Mullane met one of the Ballygunner officers and shouldered him against the wall of the tunnel coming out.

We started Mullane midfield – he probably never played there before – for about six or seven minutes. We got a good enough start and there was pandemonium. We were flying. Winning every ball, first to the ball, the appetite was good, the hurling was good.

When you beat somebody by 15 points and have to play them again later on in a county final, there's definitely going to be a touch of complacency. And remember this was a De La Salle team that won the championship two years earlier. They weren't rookies. It was an absolute hiding.

3-13 to 1-11.

Stephen Daniels was Man of the Match.

He was somebody that got everybody going. They called him Danno. He raised the spirits of everybody when he caught a high ball or flattened a fella with a belt of a shoulder or crashed into a tackle. He was a folk hero. He tore into it. No holds barred. He fought like a tiger. Brave, a good hurler and a really nice guy.

Kevin Moran was centre-back on that team. Phelan was a really good hurler as well but he didn't realise how good he was and sometimes bothered about small things. Before a match, he would be up to 90 and doubting himself but he played some great games. Remember that point in the 2009 All-Ireland semi-final against Cushendall to draw the match!

Dean Twomey got his chance that particular year. A very talented player in the middle of the field. Then you had the county guys. We made the full-back, Ian Flynn captain. He was a real warrior. He didn't collect prisoners. He wouldn't have been the fanciest hurler around but he was a real tough, honest as could be, unassuming guy who loved the club.

We had two good corner-backs, Michael Doherty and Darren Russell. Two quick nippy corner-backs. Stevie Brenner was in goal. We had Phelan, Kevin and Daniels; that was a serious defence when you add it all up. Conan Watt could run all day. Eoin Madigan and Jake Dillon came onto the team. They were only young fellas. They were only minors.

Eoin Madigan was a big lad. We had the experience from the previous two years and we had the hunger. I remember the buzz on the pitch first of all and in the dressing-room after the match. It was just magic.

We went for a few drinks. We came down again the following day!

We knew we had a right chance of winning Munster.

We played the Cork champions, Sarsfields in Páirc Uí Chaoimh. Away from home, it didn't bother us. We were in a good place. We had beaten them two years before that. The place was buzzing, everyone was looking forward to it. The feeling was we had beaten these before, we can beat them again.

It was a cracking match, and we won it after extra-time. Fellas like Mullane and Moran could do something special, and Moran was outstanding that day.

Moran brought the match to extra-time. That was some score. He must have been a 100 yards out. That was one of the greatest scores in the history of the Munster Club Championship.

Moran was majestic. I thought that his best position for the club was centre-back and his best position for the county was left half-back. I know he played outstanding games at midfield but I thought he could really control a game in the half-back line. He always used the ball really well. He was very strong in the air as well.

Once we got it to extra-time, I felt the momentum was with us. I didn't think during the course of the 60 minutes we had played as well as we could play. We were coming into it after winning three games relatively easy so nothing prepares you for it.

Mullane wouldn't have been De La Salle's free taker before that; it was our decision to put him on the frees. We didn't have a nine out of 10 free taker. We looked at a few options and we felt it might be good for him. Phelan was a great option on long range frees.

There was nothing flash about that team. You had half a dozen fellas who weren't the best hurlers on the planet but they'd give you every ounce they had. They would chase, tackle, hook and block. Those guys loved the battle, they wouldn't shy away from it. There was no shirker on that team, everyone would put their shoulder to the wheel. They had huge pride in playing for De La Salle. They loved the club.

Then we played Thurles Sarsfields in the Munster final at Páirc Uí Chaoimh. That was the morning of the frost.

There were people who couldn't get their cars out of their driveways in Waterford. If the driveway was uphill, they couldn't move their cars at all, the frost was so bad. I was at a ladies football All Star function in Dublin the night before. I left early and drove home after it.

Everyone knew it was going to be very frosty.

I met the bus at the Park Hotel in Dungarvan. We were wondering would the match be played at all. A few messages went out for people to leave on time. The bus man wanted plenty of time.

We travelled to Cork and we looked at the pitch and under the stand it was rock hard. It was so bad that we considered wearing a blade and a stud, one of each to see could we get a grip.

Would it be feasible to wear one of each?

We didn't do it but we spoke about it. The stand side was dangerous, now. Depending where you were on the pitch, you could go from frozen to soft.

Sars were cocky. They were red hot favourites.

No one gave us a chance, only ourselves.

One thing we did speak about in the two weeks before the match was nobody was to drop the ball on top of Padraic Maher. He was centre-back and he was like a lighthouse. I think it only happened twice in the match.

It was nine points to eight. I didn't care if it was 2-1!

I remember after the game John Keane was absolutely thrilled. He was a Borris-Ileigh man, five or six miles out the road! To beat Sars in a final!

We held Lar Corbett to one point. They had 17 wides.

You get nothing for putting the ball wide!

I don't think they were complacent, I just think we outfought them, we outmuscled them. A lot of those wides were under extreme pressure, now. The tackling was great. We pulled everyone back a line and we kept our defence nice and compact. We didn't want space in front of Lar and Pa Bourke.

Brian Phelan poleaxed Alan Kennedy with a belt of a shoulder. That was a pivotal moment in that game. It was a serious collision. He shook everything that was inside in him with the belt. It was an honest belt of a shoulder, no dirt.

John Sexton was appointed as referee. I heard his father had passed away and I thought he wouldn't be doing the game. I remember meeting him under the stand before the match and shaking hands with him. I couldn't believe it. I was very happy to see him refereeing because he was a very honest guy and he wasn't swayed by big names – and they had a few big stars playing.

I was delighted. I remember looking out on the pitch and looking at him blowing the whistle for a minute's silence for his father. It was a poignant moment.

Jesus this never happened before.

It was nice in a way that he went ahead and did the game. He never gave soft frees and let it flow. Conditions were dreadful and fellas were going to be slipping and sliding.

People won't regard that as the best game but we didn't give a damn. We just wanted to win the Munster Championship. Because we knew if we won that Munster Championship we had a right chance at winning the All-Ireland.

WE WERE TRAINING just after Christmas and it was going very poorly. John Keane got a ball, went on a solo run and I blew the whistle and he drove the ball out into the next field! Miles away!

The next thing Mullane and Brian Phelan tore into one another. Fisticuffs.

'Leave them at it,' I said.

We left them at it for about a minute, and they slogged it out and then they stopped. Then we had a chat and I said to John Keane, 'Go and get that ball you hit away'.

We had a fantastic training session after that, everybody had a good laugh and the whole year took off again.

We trained in Piltown under lights because there were no lights in De La Salle. About a week before the All-Ireland semi-final, we brought down Jimmy Barry-Murphy for a session. It wasn't rocket science. It was a simple hurling session; he gave a talk to the players and then we were ready.

Clarinbridge. All-Ireland semi-final.

Up in Thurles on a perfect day.

The story going into that game was… 'At least it isn't Portumna'.

My line to the players was… 'Portumna were in the Galway Championship and this team won it. At this moment in time… they're better than Portumna'.

The game was to and fro. We went ahead, they went ahead. Eoin Madigan scored a point from the sideline, a serious point. Brian Phelan pointed a free to bring it to extra-time. I felt good about it.

All year he had been doing it.

I couldn't have asked for any more out of the players that day.

Clarinbridge never gave up.

I often heard of the word ricochet. I always associated ricochet with a John Wayne movie with a bullet. It was the first time I ever saw a real ricochet on a hurling pitch.

The ball ricocheted up off Ian Flynn's hurley, and Éanna Murphy pulled on it. He reacted very quickly. Like lightning.

3-22 to 1-27.

We scored 1-27 and lost. They got three goals.

I feel well enough to look at the last goal now.

'That game will be on TV Christmas Day,' Derek McGrath said after the match. It was scant consolation.

I was almost in a daze.

It was like losing a relative.

It was a real car crash. It was just a shock.

Being so close… *If we got a replay, even.*

It was just horrific.

I don't think you ever get over that.

In men's sport that was the toughest defeat I ever had. Definitely. It was gone past the minute of added time when they got the goal. In fairness, referees always add on two minutes anyway. No crib about that. James McGrath was the referee, another fella I got to know well in Westmeath.

But that was tough. That was a savage defeat. Savage.

To see the dressing-room after. There wasn't a word said. It was like being at a very sad funeral. There wasn't a single word. You could hear a pin fall. People didn't move in the dressing-room after the match.

Eventually I spoke. It was just shock. But that's life.

The following day I got into the car and I drove down to Wexford Park. Wexford and Waterford in the National League. I was sitting below in the stand and my phone rang. Strange number.

Micheál Donoghue.

The Clarinbridge manager. He picked up the phone and rang me. I thought that was a fantastic gesture. He didn't have to do that.

He thanked me for the game and said he knew how I was feeling. We kept in touch every now and again after that. I rang him when he got the Galway job to wish him the best of luck, and Galway played Westmeath, when I was manager there, a couple of times as well.

We felt bad that day, we felt an awful lot worse a couple of weeks later.

Clarinbridge won the final by 12 points against O'Loughlin Gaels. Double scores. Nicky Cashin rang me the night after that semi-final and he said, 'They'll win it because this is not a vintage year for Kilkenny club hurling' – and he was right. No Waterford club had ever won it.

My initial term with De La Salle was only for one year.

The Waterford job was in the back of my mind.

« CHAPTER 21 »

I THREW MY name into the hat for Waterford manager in 2010. I did an interview.

I was there in 2007 and '08, and we had a great time in '07. I knew a lot of the players. It was something I felt I wanted to do. I think Vincent Hogan gave me a scorching in the *Irish Independent*. I rang him to let him know my name was in the hat. It was something I always wanted to do anyway.

I don't think I was well enough prepared for the interview. There was a lot of things happening at the time. De La Salle were preparing for the Munster club. I didn't think it through well enough. Davy Fitzgerald got the job again and that's fair enough too because they did win the Munster Championship with Davy in 2010.

Davy is a fella I almost got to like over the years.

Having met him on the sideline with Westmeath and Waterford, you'd have to, there's something about him. Some people don't like him but he's a really good manager. He's getting better as the years go on.

I had a strong management team going in the following year. I was better prepared.

I put my name forward because Paul Flynn rang me.

'Are you going for the Waterford job?'

'I don't know,' I said.

'Why?'

'I don't know do I care.'

'Somebody better care,' he said. 'You should go for it.'

I thought about it for a day or two and then I said I would.

I knew second time around I would have to get a really good management team. It's hard to get selectors in Waterford. It's a huge commitment. I rang Nicky Cashin and he said no, that he had done it. I went down and met him and he again said no. Nicky was very disappointed with what happened with Justin. I respected that.

About two weeks later, he rang me. 'Do you still want me as a selector?'

I said I did.

Nicky was a top guy. He wouldn't be afraid to have a go at a player. Nicky had the St Kieran's and Kilkenny mentality.

Me and Nicky were there in 2007 and '08. Some players probably wouldn't have been happy about it. I think what the players wanted was probably an outsider like Anthony Daly. A big high-profile name and that didn't happen. I know they wanted a big name.

The biggest problem is the world is so impatient that everybody wants huge big names. Someone's mind is almost made up about a man or woman, before they start. If he's not high profile, it works against him. It probably worked against me that I wasn't massively high profile.

Whereas, when Davy came in, he was high profile as a player anyway even though he didn't have much managerial experience. I wasn't aware of it at the time, it's only looking back on it after.

I RANG PAT Flanagan.

I had always been aware of him. He was a Waterford man and I had seen what he had done with the Kerry footballers. I listened to a few of his interviews and I liked his bustling style. Wherever he went, he always meant business.

'Michael Ryan here… you don't know me. I'm going for the Waterford manager's job, would you like to help Waterford win an All-Ireland?'

He chuckled.

'Go on… talk away,' he said.

'I'll go up and meet you… when are you free?'

I drove to meet him in Tralee.

'Park your car, I'll take you out to where I live,' he said.

He was living up in the hills between Tralee and Killarney. Just as I got into his car, his phone rang. It was Declan Ryan, the Tipperary manager!

'I can't talk... I'm with somebody now.'

'You've competition,' he said to me.

'That's what I like... competition!'

We drove down to his house and I spoke to him for two hours. After two hours, he said, 'Look, why don't you get this fella or that fella'.

'If I wanted this fella or that fella... I wouldn't be here. I want you to do this job and I'm not leaving here until you say yes.'

His daughter Aoife was walking across with two cups of tea. 'Dad you're always talking about it so just go and do it.'

His wife Ann Marie was upstairs, she was studying for a PhD.

She came down.

'This man wants me to go to Waterford,' Pat said to her.

'Why don't you go?'

I piped up.

'Pat... your daughter says yes, your wife says yes.'

We spoke for another hour and he said, 'Yes'.

Brother Philip Ryan was on board as well as a selector.

I released my management team to the press then! Gordon Manning, the GAA writer, was a friend of mine. I felt that with a strong management team, I had a better chance of getting the job.

I was asked about it at the interview.

'Did you release it to the press?'

'No.'

'How did they find out?'

'How do I know?'

So, I'm guilty on all counts!

While I was with De La Salle, we did a lot of video analysis – Ken Cullinane did it for me. He was brilliant at it. He had a mini-cinema built into his house so I often went through stuff with him into the early hours of the morning.

When I got the Waterford job, something happened and I was told that I couldn't have Ken Cullinane with me.

I wanted to have him because I felt he was very good at video analysis, but I wasn't allowed to have him.

I did a PowerPoint presentation. I was better prepared. I had more time to do it. I wasn't in the middle of a Munster club campaign.

I was called back for a second interview.

Again, I felt it went okay. I was driving out by the Touraneena GAA pitch and the phone rang. It was Timmy O'Keeffe, the county secretary.

'You have the job. Don't tell anybody… we have to ring the other candidates.'

There I was.

Waterford manager. There was no fanfare. I went home and we went up to Doocey's for a few pints.

I felt it was my time. A lot of people would have said it to me over the years. 'Would you ever throw your name in the hat?'

I was made very aware of the budget from day one. Expenses had to be tightened up. Paddy Joe Ryan told me, 'Don't spare spending on the players, because the players won't thank you for it'. Ultimately, he was proved right.

When I came before the committee, I told them I was going to get Pat Flanagan down from Kerry. I sorted out his travel expenses, which weren't extravagant. I got that funded. I had a good relationship with Club Déise.

They funded a training camp down in Fota Island. Money was very tight. That was made absolutely clear. I sat down with Timmy and went through our budget. Everything had to be cut back. The spending of previous years couldn't continue.

Things like gear; I wouldn't say we skimped on it but there was no extravagance. And tickets for matches. In fairness to the players – we carried 35 on the panel – they agreed to take three tickets each, instead of four, so that everybody else would get them.

There wasn't a problem with that, the players were very good from that point of view. Travel expenses were a matter between the board and the players. Jim Dee would have done that; he was great to work with. He was fair.

Pat Moore was our goalkeeping coach and he was excellent. I felt that he should have been in charge of underage coaching in Waterford.

Money was scarce. Simple. The fact of it is that a couple of years later, when Paddy Joe Ryan came in as chairman, Waterford were in debt. That didn't happen during my reign, that was built up over many years before that.

Paddy Joe again sorted out the county board finances. He had originally turned around a huge deficit in the 1990s.

We did our best to keep a tight rein on finances but ultimately players won't thank you for that. Like, there was no other way to do it. There's no point spending money and the county board writing a cheque, and the cheque bouncing. I always felt that the board did their best. Timmy was very straight. I found him good to work with. There were no grey areas with Timmy. His role was to curtail things and keep a handle on things as well.

Around that time, right around the country, there seemed to be an explosion of travel expenses. People suddenly started to throw massive money at county teams. Mayo, Dublin, Cork… Kilkenny.

The budgets exploded; they went through the roof at a time when Waterford were cutting back. Everything is relative. You take Kilkenny.

Every player in Kilkenny is probably within 20 miles of Nowlan Park. It's right in the centre of the county.

All those things are going to help.

WE MET EOIN Kelly at the start of pre-season and we gave him a programme to go away and get fit.

We realised that he was a really good player but he was only a really good player if he was fit. It was an attempt to give him a reality check. We told him that we would assess him again and review it.

We decided to give him a jolt and try to get more out of him.

No good saying it worked, it didn't work. He didn't respond in the way we thought he might. When he came back in, he didn't show any signs of improvement. I think he found it hard to train on his own. It didn't work for him.

Eventually, we reviewed it again and we invited him back. It wasn't going to resolve itself. I must say when he came back in, he did make a serious effort. He bought into it and trained really hard.

He came on in the league game against Dublin, made the team for the championship and was instrumental in beating Clare. He was a bit of a genius but sometimes he didn't work as hard as he could have worked. Some talent. He could do things with a ball that other people could only dream about.

WE INSISTED ON the gym sessions being supervised.

I don't think the players were happy about that. Every gym session was supervised in Waterford and Clonea. I'd seen it with another county team, they were in the sauna when they were supposed to be in the gym.

Jimmy Payne was in Waterford, Pat Flanagan was in Clonea. Pat used to leave Tralee at two o'clock, drive to Waterford for training and drive back again. Three times a week.

Everything was supervised. Maybe the players felt they weren't being trusted. We had to be sure. There was probably 90 percent of them that could be trusted but there was always 10 percent that couldn't be. We wanted to make sure that they all bought in.

Then, we got a bad start to the year.

2012 National Hurling League.

Cork 3-17 Waterford 0-18.

Kilkenny 2-21 Waterford 1-15.

Tipperary 0-31 Waterford 2-15

We had a whole load of injuries for the first couple of league games. We had Cork away with Jimmy Barry-Murphy as manager. The messiah returning.

Páirc Uí Rinn full.

Ten thousand people. The game was live on television. They were putting the ball over the bar from the dressing-room!

We were missing several players, including John Mullane, Tony Browne, Eoin Kelly, Noel Connors, Stephen O'Keeffe, Shane O'Sullivan, Richie Foley, Aidan Kearney and Maurice Shanahan.

Shane Walsh and Shane Casey went off injured.

With that many players gone, we didn't have a chance.

Would any county manager survive if there were 12 players gone?

NOBODY IS GOING to be singing your praises after losing three matches.

I did an interview with WLR after the Tipperary game in Semple Stadium. 'The biggest worry I have is that we are not playing well all over the field. We are just not up to the pace of the game, we don't look sharp… we don't look fit and we don't look mentally focussed and that's something the management must sort out.'

Jackie Cahill wrote an article. If I remember correctly, the headline was…

Ryan lashes Waterford players.

I didn't realise that he didn't write the headline.

I rang Jackie

'Jackie… what I said was everybody needs to step up to the plate here, players and management. We must all take the blame and we must all respond.'

Jackie said that he didn't write the headline.

'Jackie don't you ever again ring me for an article.'

He said that I couldn't do that.

'You watch me.'

There was a cooling off with Jackie and myself!

I met Jackie later on at the launch of DJ Carey's book. We were sitting at the same table. We had a chat and we moved on. I accepted that he hadn't written the headline.

I'd been brought up with the media as regards ladies football but this was a different level of it. I always believed in listening to the question, taking three or four seconds before I answered, weigh it up and be honest, tell the truth.

The one thing I learned, as a county manager, is that there's no room for grey areas or loose remarks because somebody will interpret them in a way that'll come back to cause trouble. You have to be very careful with every single thing you say, and who you say it to.

You can't even speak on the street because by the time it's got back, there'll be 14 and a half legs on it!

A million times worse and certainly taken out of context.

WE REALISED WE weren't going well.

We asked the players to have a meeting before training one night.

I don't know how long it lasted.

We had a chat and then we left it to the players to have a chat. Stephen Molumphy spoke to the media the following day and said we know what we have to do.

We played Brick in the forwards in the first couple of games and he played well there. The problem was we had no other centre-back. It wasn't that he was doing anything wrong in the forwards.

Brick was a serious leader.

No player in this country has fulfilled his potential as much as Brick.

Brick wasn't the best hurler on the planet but he always managed to get the very best out of himself. When he hung up those boots, he could say he couldn't have done anymore. That's a test of any player.

There's loads of good players around the world who waste their talent.

Brick made sure nobody got carried away, particularly players. I remember the first night Jamie Barron came into training down in WIT. Brick flattened him twice. He absolutely flattened him, now. Jamie bounced up and I remember Brick saying after, 'He'll be okay!' He tested young players to see were they up for it. He never wanted limelight, even when he was appointed captain.

He was a shy kind of a guy, shy in the sense that he shunned publicity. When the ball was thrown in, the shyness went out the window.

He wouldn't say an awful lot but his timing was very good. He seemed to wait until the dust was on the way back down again. The dust rises and then it comes back down again! He came in then with his three or four sentences.

He was the master of being down to earth.

NICKY CASHIN HAD enough. When things aren't going well, it isn't easy. He had been down that road before.

I'm still good friends with Nicky, we keep in touch.

I remember we were training in Carriganore and a fella abused Nicky. I couldn't believe it. We had played no match. This fella absolutely laid into Nicky. For no reason. I just couldn't believe it.

Why I don't know. Nicky was surprised. I was surprised.

He just had enough. He was very disappointed that a supporter should come and challenge him in an aggressive way.

There was a lot of criticism coming after losing three matches. Nicky didn't want it and I'd say Brother Philip didn't want it either. We were well beaten in those games. The only thing I was praying for was to get some of the injured fellas back. We couldn't afford to be without some of our best players.

Nicky stepped away and Brother Philip stepped away.

So there I was, no selectors… just Pat and myself.

The biggest problem I found with Waterford – and other managers have said it to me since – was to get selectors to commit to the county set-up. There's so much time involved. I spoke to Stephen Frampton at the time and he couldn't commit.

It's like everything else, your first day in the job isn't going to be your best day. Your first month isn't going to be your best month. There's always lessons to be learned and you have to learn them and learn them very quickly.

Anything you do wrong is going to be magnified.

If things don't work out, the blame is always going to come back on the manager. The players don't usually get the blame.

The biggest lesson of all was winning matches.

If you don't start winning matches, it doesn't make a difference who you are… you're in trouble.

« CHAPTER 22 »

Only woe so far for Waterford manager, Michael Ryan, selector resigning, his young side really struggling for consistency. In John Mullane and Eoin Kelly they'll have a couple of experienced forwards around this week to steady the ship, but currently they're floundering.

— Diarmuid O'Flynn, *Irish Examiner*, March 24, 2012

I HAD TO find results.

Pat Grant told me that we had to stay in Division 1.

If we didn't stay in Division 1, my job was in jeopardy. Which is a bit odd, because two years later Waterford got relegated and it made no difference.

Where that came from, I don't know. I never let it worry me anyway. I said I'd do my best, fight on and see what happens. It didn't keep me awake at night.

There was a lot of flak.

I probably wasn't getting it because I wasn't in the city. I never bothered about the flak because I had been getting it all my life.

I wouldn't be a fella for reading newspapers.

People would tell me this or that when I met them, or the family would tell me at home. I didn't read it; I didn't take any notice of it. I didn't care what was on the paper. I saw some of it but I made a conscious decision for it not to bother me.

You're always under pressure managing a county team. My attitude was… *I'll give this everything I have and I can do no more.*

Whatever will be will be.

That's always been my attitude to any job I've taken.

Ken McGrath came in as a selector. I met him in his own house. His brother, Eoin sounded him out. He said he'd think about it. He rang me back a day or two later and said he'd give it a go.

He came in and he was a massive man to have around the team. He was well respected and he was great around the place.

In my opinion, Ken McGrath is the best hurler Waterford ever had. He did it everywhere. He started off as a wing forward, he got seven points from play when they won the Munster final, then he went back in the backs. Ken was a big influence around the team.

It was a pity he didn't stay on in some fashion the following year.

Séan Cullinane came in as well.

We were under massive pressure going to Galway. Ken was on the sideline but he couldn't really act because he wasn't ratified. That's the politics of the GAA! He came up the day of the game.

We had a good team meeting on the Saturday night. We asked for a response. The only two mentors that were at it were Pat Flanagan and myself. Ken wasn't ratified, Brother Philip came to Galway but stepped down after the game and Nicky Cashin had already stepped down.

John Mullane came as well. He was thinking of coming back to the panel and he did. I said to Mullane that we were down a lot of fellas. He rang me back and said he'd travel.

Mullane was a fella that liked to be right. He never wanted to play if he wasn't fit. He wasn't a fella who would play for the sake of playing. It was a massive fillip for us. He was huge that day.

We met Galway on one of those days when Galway weren't at their best. Part of that was the fact that we tore into the fray from the start.

Shane Walsh shouldered James Skehill in the act of scoring a goal and the goalie broke his collarbone. The team just took off, they started hurling well.

We rolled up the sleeves and tore into Galway.

Everybody was hurt. The players were hurt, the management were hurt.

We asked for a response and they certainly gave a response. We beat Galway

1-14 to 0-15 and straight away there was a weight lifted off everybody. It was a huge relief. That was a Galway team that was in the All-Ireland final later that year.

Reports of our death were greatly exaggerated!

Suddenly it was in our own hands to stay in the division. We had Dublin in Fraher Field. We knew if we won that game, we were in fourth place. We had a few fellas back so training was a bit better. Ken took a lot of the sessions.

He was great. He wouldn't have been into all those mad tactics but I wouldn't say he had no tactics. He was a bit like Michael Walsh of Kilkenny. Michael's philosophy is, the ball to play is the intelligent ball, whether that be short or long.

The intelligent ball.

Ken did the coaching, Séan gave a hand and Pat and Jimmy Payne did the strength and conditioning. We always sat down and prepared. We often met on nights when there was no training on.

As a management team, we would plan the night's session. My job would be to observe it, look around and see what's happening; make sure that Pat got his time and Ken got his time. Anyone who's injured is with the physio and all the other things that go with it.

I'd always find time at training to talk to three or four players, you can't talk to everybody on any given night. If somebody didn't have a good game or if somebody was injured or if somebody wasn't playing well, you'd pull them away and have a chat and try and get inside their head.

Because if you don't know what's going on inside their head or don't know what the problem is, it's very hard to fix it. The only way to find out that is to talk to the players.

A million meetings go on.

Media duties, county board… gear.

At the end of the day, any county manager is responsible for 50 or 60 people. That's a full-time job. You don't have time to coach.

It's something I've been doing all my life, I just always find time. If you want something done, ask somebody that's busy because that's the reason they're busy. How many hours went into it never bothered me.

I've always felt that there's four or five players on any panel that you can talk to, suss things out and find out exactly what the mood is. You have to know, to some extent, what the players are thinking.

Then you go back and talk about it as a management team and assess the players.

We had so many meetings, particularly Pat and myself. Jimmy Payne was there as well. And selectors meetings. We had a review of every single thing but at the end of the day, the manager carries the can.

I can't speak for the players but I would have felt that the players weren't happy with themselves or with the management after losing the first three league games. I would've guessed that. After that, the training got better.

I would have felt communication was okay. I don't think it's ever going to be perfect because at the end of the day, you take any panel. You have 35 players, there's 20 of them unhappy straight away. Fifty percent of the players are always going to be unhappy. It only takes a very small swing then to tilt the ship or the balance of power.

I did notice that the training got better after winning the game in Galway. Everybody seemed happy, everybody worked harder. Once we started winning, the players saw it in a different light.

Mullane was a massive help as well.

There was Fergie Time and there was Mullane Time.

Before he went out, he would walk around the dressing-room and throw out a few expletives. It was his way of psyching himself up.

He had this habit of slapping the back of his legs.

'When are we going out?'

Ten minutes before we went out on the field, he would get up, start hopping the hurley off the back of his legs, redden his legs and walk around the dressing-room. He went into a different mode.

There was a table and Roger Casey's hand was up on the table. Roger was the kitman.

'F*** these Dubs!'

He pulled down on top of the table across Roger's hand.

Mullane never even knew he hit him!

As the game started, I looked behind me and there was our physio and our doctor trying to patch up Roger's hand in the dugout. He was very badly bruised.

We brought on Eoin Kelly and he got a marvellous point.

We won 0-17 to 0-13 and we finished fourth in Division 1. There were only six teams. It was cutthroat.

We had a training camp in Fota and we all put a lot of work into that. That seemed to go very well.

We dropped Tony Browne for the Munster semi-final against Clare. That was a tough call. Tony had been struggling. We told him together as a management. The three of us. Any fella who was left off, we told him.

I would never let a fella find out in front of 30 people that he was being dropped. Nobody is happy to be dropped but in fairness he accepted it. He won his place back for the Munster final. That's the kind of man he was. Tony was such a good wing back that the onus was nearly on the wing forward to mark him. He was a really top player.

Tony was different.

He liked the chance to prepare himself and Justin afforded him that chance. We got him to do more early in the season than he did in previous years. Even when he was dropped, he bounced back. To play to the level he did, at the age he was, he seemed to be almost like a full-time, professional hurler, the way he prepared. He left no stone unturned to make sure that he was completely mentally and physically right himself.

The championship draw was made the previous October and I knew we were going to draw Clare. It was bound to happen. The Davy factor was coming down the track and that was going to be a distraction in itself.

That was going to take on a life of its own.

We stopped in Clonmel for a pre-match meal, we had a meeting in the hotel. I always believe that when you're talking to players, you must pull something out. You must have something different every time you speak. I had heard a story that the Clare players were brought out of bed one morning and made climb Carrauntohill.

'This is what we're up against today.

'Listen very carefully.

'About six weeks ago, the Clare players got a phone call after midnight to be in Cusack Park an hour later… where they were met by a bus. They drove through the darkness of the night and they went to Kerry and they climbed Carrauntohill.

'All the ways up and all the ways down again.'

Everyone was looking at me.

'In the middle of the night.'

I left it hang there.

There was a lot of tension about the match because these fellas wanted to beat Davy.

'Climbing up mountains makes you good at…

'Climbing up mountains!'

The whole place erupted! It lifted the tension.

Stephen O'Keeffe, Stephen Daniels, Philip Mahony and Gavin O'Brien all made their championship debuts. Fourteen months later, Clare were All-Ireland champions. The Clare goalie, Patrick Kelly came up and took a free at the end and the ball ricocheted up in the air. I thought it was in the back of the net.

Stephen Molumphy came out with it.

I WASN'T HAPPY about Mullane and Kelly celebrating in front of Davy. I was disappointed it happened.

That's not my style at all. You lose with grace and you win with grace as well. But it happened and what could I do?

Of course, the media hounded me over it.

Our lads were delighted to beat Davy and delighted to get back to a Munster final again. For some of them, it was the be-all and end-all. He would have put manners on some of those fellas. They just couldn't wait to play against him.

I didn't say anything to Mullane and Kelly, there was no point because it was like throwing petrol on a fire, but I was disappointed with it. They were on a high over it. From Davy's point of view, we got a goal from a penalty that should have been a free out. Kelly pulled Cian Dillon's helmet.

One man who led the team that year was Stephen Molumphy.

Molumphy always led the way. Molumphy was a born leader. He would be a fella that would go around and say a few words to fellas privately. He wouldn't be one that wanted the whole world to know what he was doing but behind the scenes he was a guy who was born to lead.

It probably came from his work in the army.

He was with that Ballyduff Upper team that won the county in 2007 against all the odds.

THE MUNSTER FINAL was against Tipp, who had beaten us by 21 points the previous year. We felt that we'd give Tipp a game.

There was a lot of talk about playing in Cork. We had been hammered in Cork. We had a vote amongst the players. Were they prepared to go to Thurles for the Munster final? Out of the panel of 30… 25 or 26 of them said yes.

It never came to anything.

It was a drizzly kind of a day. We hurled well enough.

We gave away two poorish goals. They beat us by seven. We never looked like winning but it could have been a three-point game.

It was a decent performance without setting the world on fire. I wouldn't be calling it a moral victory, I'm not into moral victories. I remember leaving Cork saying that there's something to work with here.

WE SHOULD HAVE beaten Cork in the All-Ireland quarter-final. We were three points up and we missed a chance to go four up.

Then, they went down the field, got a point and it was back to two.

We hurled well in that game, we coped with their lively forwards. We pulled back our half-back line, we said the '45' was their bench line and pulled back the midfield a bit and crowded it up; we didn't give them much space.

Shane Casey had a chance at the end, and Eoin McGrath had a chance as well. We got a lot of criticism over playing Eoin. Ken got the blame, but I'll take responsibility for that.

He had been going well in training and if you look at the DVD of that game, I think he got five balls and did well with four of them. He just happened to miss a chance and that's what everybody remembered.

Eoin McGrath was a maligned figure. If it was raining, Eoin McGrath was blamed. But it was my call.

We wouldn't have feared Galway in the semi-final. Anything could have happened.

'Don't worry, I'll be around,' I told the reporters after the game, when I was asked about the length of my term.

I had a two-year term and that was it. I always felt that you had to kill speculation at the start. Don't give a half-hearted answer, put it to bed straight off.

After the game, we sat down as a management team and we felt we had turned a corner. We had stayed up in Division 1, got to the Munster final and should have won that Cork game. Waterford had lost a lot of players in the few years before that but we had a few new fellas coming through, and we had given championship debuts to six players.

We felt that there was plenty to work with.

« CHAPTER 23 »

IN JANUARY 2013, JOHN Mullane rang me. He was thinking of giving it up.

I met him down in the Ramada Hotel. I remember exactly where we were… inside the door on the left hand side, a table for two people.

Mullane strolls in and before he sat down, he said, 'I shouldn't be here because, to be honest, my mind is probably made up… and you could probably persuade Paisley to become a Catholic!'

That's exactly what he said to me.

We spoke for an hour. We discussed a lot of things.

We discussed his career. I told him how important he was to the team. I thought he had a bit left in him. I didn't go down on my knees and beg because I realised a long time ago that doesn't work.

'Look, I feel my time is done,' he said. 'I don't have the appetite for it anymore.'

'Okay,' I said. 'I'll ring you again in a month. If you change your mind, that's fair enough but you won't hear from me for a month… but I'll ring you once more.'

We shook hands and left.

I rang him a month later and he said he wouldn't be coming back.

I was in Clonmel when I rang him.

'No… I'm going to retire,' he said.

'That's fair enough,' I said. 'You don't owe Waterford anything.'

He just didn't have the stomach for it anymore.

He couldn't motivate himself to go back into it again. The previous year he went home in the middle of a training session. We were training really hard in Carriganore and he just didn't have the stomach for it, or the heart for it.

When you've played for a long time and you don't have the stomach for it, you just can't do it.

We let him come back late in 2012. He was probably burnt out, he was there since 2001. That was 12 seasons, playing corner-forward, getting flaked morning, noon and night. Coming up against some of the toughest defenders in the world... Brian Murphy, Jackie Tyrell... these fellas. I always had a good relationship with Mullane.

So, Mullane gave up, Philip Mahony went touring, and Molumphy went away with the army. Eoin McGrath and Eoin Kelly retired.

They were body blows now. Philip had bedded into the team really well.

KEN WAS A big loss. He got a certain amount of criticism over playing Eoin, which was my decision. He had a young family so he said that's enough.

He rang me and I knew from the tone that his mind was made up. County management is such a big deal, there's no point trying to force anybody. He admitted himself that it was an eye-opener.

'I wouldn't have your job for a million quid,' he said to me one time.

He enjoyed coaching.

Ray Murphy worked with me in De La Salle. He was a sharp guy, I felt he had something to offer to the backroom team. He was a fella that wasn't afraid to call a spade a spade. He was in no way biased towards anybody. He was always able to look at the big picture. Favouritism wasn't on his agenda.

We won our first league game against Clare.

We arrived in Ennis; we stayed the night before in Limerick. Inside the gate, above in Cusack Park, this fella came over to me in a paper cap. Clare colours.

He shook hands with me.

'I'm supporting Clare for 50 years, but I hope ye win the match... I can't stand Davy.'

I was gobsmacked.

To think that a Clare supporter would say that.

After the match, that same guy came over to me again.

'I'm delighted ye won!' I couldn't believe it! Jesus who would be a manager! When some fella from your own county says that.

Unbelievable!

That was a big one, very few teams beat them in Ennis.

'First question from me,' I asked the journalists.

'Did any of ye get a prediction right?'

There were no takers.

'Lads, no hard feelings!'

We were moving well. We were starting to play a slightly different brand of hurling. We started to play 30, 40 yard passes and clear the half-back line, because every team in the country were good in the air in the half-back line. We tried to work the ball out to midfield and by-pass the half-back line.

Some young fellas came through and started to do well. Jake Dillon was starting to find his feet.

The second game was against Cork in Dungarvan on a terrible day, around the time former Waterford manager Tony Mansfield died. Seamus Prendergast got a late point to draw the game. The weather was horrendous.

That was the worst day I ever saw for a county game.

We came back from five points down to beat Tipp in Walsh Park. Won by a point. Jamie Barron got a goal that day into the Town End. Coming in from the right wing. That was the day Jamie Barron announced himself to the world.

We played Galway in the last game and they beat us by four points, so we didn't qualify. We finished fourth twice in my time, we were never in a relegation battle but we never made the league semi-finals. In any other era, we'd have been in the league quarter-finals.

The system in those two years worked against us. You had to finish in the top three in Division 1 to get into the semi-finals.

We had another training camp down in Fota. It wasn't as good as the year before. The same thing happened with Justin when we went to Portugal. For some reason, the second time around, it never seems as good. Maybe it's because you're trying to repeat what you did before.

CLARE AGAIN IN the Munster championship.

I felt the referee was under a bit of pressure because he was the same referee that gave the penalty to Kelly the previous year. James McGrath.

In the build-up to the game, a bit had been made about the mistake he made the year before. I felt that they got some handy frees. How the GAA could give a fella the same two teams two years in-a-row beats me, but nobody should be surprised because they are capable of doing anything. James was a fella that I got to know very well after in Westmeath!

We had only six players that started against Clare the previous year.

We were four points up at half-time. We didn't take our chances.

We had 15 wides. After half-time, we had a bad spell. At a vital stage, Shane O'Donnell got a goal and they won pulling up. It opened the floodgates.

In fairness to Davy, Clare were the fittest team in the country. I just felt that we ran out of bodies to be honest. We just didn't have the bench. We lost four or five players. In my time, we never really had a full panel of players. Clare proved their mettle later on; they went on and won the All-Ireland.

Justin always said that if you're hurling well, you'll run all day. He's right. Clare were very fit. I'd always trust Pat Flanagan and Jimmy Payne.

Jimmy would have worked with Davy. Pat trained Kerry. I would argue that the fitness levels for football have to be even higher than hurling.

Now we were going to Tullamore against an Offaly team that had scored four goals against Kilkenny. I was concerned going into that game. We had a bad last 20 minutes against Clare. It would have been a disaster if we lost that game and that's no disrespect to Offaly.

We had to win.

We were playing against the wind in the second-half and we spoke about doing what we'd been doing in the league all year. We had a really good chat at half-time.

We felt that we had to use the ball well, quieten the crowd and sow the seed of doubt. I remember talking to the Offaly manager, Ollie Baker after and he said in the first 15 minutes of the second-half we quenched them. We used that ball very well; we controlled that game. We won by four, but I felt we were more than four points the better team.

Maurice Shanahan really cut loose... 13 points.

He had a mighty game. A good lad, a nice fella. He was always living in the shadow of Dan but a very good hurler and a great club hurler. We were delighted to get out of that.

We played Westmeath the following week. There was a strong wind in Mullingar. At half-time, the game was in the melting pot. We spoke at half-time about the need to up our game all over the pitch. In the second-half, Brian O'Sullivan got a pair of goals.

Maurice got 1-9 even though Westmeath people tell me they held him! Tony Browne came on and he left his hurley on the pitch after the game. There was a bit of an SOS to find it but we found it eventually.

We'd won two championship games, and were heading for Kilkenny, and there was no reason to be optimistic outside our camp.

But we felt that we had a chance.

I WAS CONFIDENT going into that game. You know from training.

Training well, hurling well, confident.

A buzz around the place, and everybody really ready for the challenge.

The plan was we'd work the ball through the lines and keep it away from their half-back line. We picked Darragh Fives at midfield; we felt that he was capable of scoring from out the field. We decided that whatever happens we can't drop the ball on top of their half-back line or they'd slaughter us.

By and large, it worked.

We were ready to come out on the pitch and we had to go back in again because the other game went to extra-time between Wexford and Clare. That threw us a bit.

We had a goal chance early on.

Maurice put Jamie in, but he missed it. It was his first championship season. We were hurling really well all over the pitch.

At half-time, we were confident. We had the legs.

We weren't one bit intimidated by them. They were making a good few positional switches. Brian Cody brought on Henry Shefflin, and took him off again. Kevin Moran got a brilliant point from the right wing under the stand to bring us level. We got the last five points in normal time.

And then we had a chance.

The ball came to Paudie Prendergast. I don't know was he trying to find Seamus inside or going for a score. A draw. 0-15 to 1-12.

We were confident heading into extra-time that we had a good chance. Richie Hogan caused the damage. Four points.

He was the difference.

We lost 1-22 to 2-16.

There's not one fella on that Kilkenny team that day who wasn't a household name. That team were reigning All-Ireland champions and won the next two titles in 2014 and '15. Look at the list of changes they made.

Henry Shefflin taken off… Michael Rice taken off… Aidan Fogarty taken off… Walter Walsh taken off. Brought on fellas, took off fellas.

Martin O'Neill came on for us and got injured. Cruciate. We timed it afterwards, he was on the pitch for 45 seconds. Losing Darragh Fives was a big blow because he was really hurling well. He got three points. He got a bang on the leg. What might have been!

I went into their dressing-room and I was walking down to our dressing-room and Brian Cody said, 'I thought we were gone!'

If we had beaten Kilkenny, we were in a good place.

Looking back on it, we had to beat them in normal time.

I was made aware of an interview Mullane did with Newstalk.

I was open to a phone call but that phone call never came.

I stressed in the build-up to the Kilkenny game that it was the one game that I possibly would have liked to have played.

That's what John Mullane said on *Off The Ball*.

We weren't playing a game of cards. He just couldn't come down from the stand and play against Kilkenny, the All-Ireland champions, without serious preparation… and he didn't have that preparation.

I wasn't aware of it until after.

Even if I was aware of it, you just can't do that. We weren't going for a game of 45! We were playing the best team in the country, the best team that ever played the game. Having said that, if we had a fully fit John Mullane it probably would have tilted it for us.

You just can't come down from the middle of the stand and trot out and play hurling when you haven't trained with the county for six months. There's no point going through the motions.

ABOVE ALL THE games I was ever involved in, the feed-back from the supporters was incredible. A lot of people loved the style of hurling we played that night.

I felt it was the start of something.

Again, I was asked about my future by the reporters.

'My name will be in the hat as I imagine will the rest of the management team.'

« CHAPTER 24 »

Michael Ryan has officially informed Waterford Co Board that he will not be seeking the position of Senior Hurling Team Manager for 2014

@WaterfordGAA August 11, 2013

WHEN THE TITANIC left Belfast, it was in a good place and when I left Waterford hurling, it was in a good place as well.

My reaction then and now is one of disappointment.

What disappointed me most was the fact that we had produced Waterford's best display in a long time, with a lot of good young players coming through, and we didn't get a chance to work with them for another year.

We had a decent year.

In the league, we beat Tipp, beat Clare away and drew with Cork. Disappointed with the Clare game, even though Clare deserved to beat us, they were very fit.

Offaly was a test, we were always going to beat Westmeath; Kilkenny had a full deck, we drew with them, could have beaten them, beat us in extra-time. I was saying that I must be doing something right, and the whole thing was starting to come together, particularly with the brand of hurling we played on the day.

I felt that we were in a good place.

If you were to ask me what progress Waterford made in the next two or three years, I didn't see much progress.

It disappointed me to hear about what Derek McGrath inherited.

That was nothing to do with Derek, that was the general commentary from people.

Derek inherited a team that nearly beat Kilkenny, who went on to win the next two All-Irelands. That's the reality of it. He also had fellas like Tadhg De Burca, Austin Gleeson and other players coming through. That's what he inherited. He didn't inherit a team that was getting beaten out the gate.

I inherited a team that was beaten in a Munster final by 21 points.

That annoyed me.

THE PROBLEM WITH the whole thing is that with every bit of controversy, people take sides. It depends on which side you're on.

The truth is probably somewhere in the middle if you understand me.

I had seen a lot of things happen over the years with different teams, different set-ups and different counties. I had seen what happened with various managers around the country. There's a load of fellas that it has happened to.

That seemed to be the trend. Players turning on managers. Go back to the start of the noughties, in those dozen years it was ripe and rampant, and it seemed to be happening in clubs as well.

THERE WERE STORIES of players being phoned up who weren't at the Waterford players' meeting that ousted me. There were only 11 players at the meeting.

I would have been talking to the Fourmilewater players, but Jamie Barron and Shane Walsh weren't at the meeting because they were playing that match with The Nire in the Millfield while the meeting was going on which is surprising. That was the system that was chosen.

Very seldom have I bumped into any of the players since.

I've met the Fives brothers a few times. I would have a good relationship with them. We wouldn't have a conversation about that but I've always got on well with Darragh and Shane. I've never really had a conversation with any other players since.

I just haven't met them.

I will say that we are probably at the stage now where the players must have some say in who the manager is. I will say that. At the end of the day, if players are going to commit five nights a week, there's no point having somebody if they're not happy with him. But there has to be a fine line as well.

The manager can't be taking all the blame for everything that goes wrong. At the end of the day, most problems are fixed on the pitch.

I met Davy at the Munster awards night up in Kerry. We were just talking for a minute and he said, 'Tis easier dealing with young lads'.

The point he made was you have more control over young lads.

I WOULDN'T SAY my record was brilliant but if you go back and take the first three games out of it, when we were missing 12 players, it was decent after that.

The biggest regret was the Cork game in 2012, and the Clare game the following year. We could have easily won those two games.

The issue was they wanted a change and they wanted a fresh voice.

You'd always do something differently.

I had asked Derek to come on board as a coach the first time. He was ambitious. He stood for manager. He was a contender when I got the job. He said he was ambitious and he wanted to get experience by standing for it.

When Derek went for the job the second time, I spoke to him and I suggested to him to do a PowerPoint presentation. The second time I did a PowerPoint presentation.

Did I give it all I had? I did.

Was I successful? So, so.

It's very hard to judge it because I felt it should have gone another year. It mightn't have worked out. It wouldn't have worked out any worse than 2014 did anyway because that was a terrible year for Waterford.

We would have been looking at some of the older players and saying their time was up. We would have been thinking about some fellas. We had spoken about that, that we needed to change things up, but never really pinpointed who. We felt with some of the players that their time was up.

In Waterford, the pool isn't that big.

So there I was, two years done. And gone.

EVER SINCE THAT day, there's not one week that goes by that people don't tell me how disappointed they were. I'm still meeting people giving out about that decision. Not alone from Waterford, from all over the country.

I parked my van in Clonmel about two months after the saga ended.

It was raining and this car pulled up beside me when I was getting out of the van and the passenger window rolled down.

This fella leaned across and put out his hand. It was Babs Keating.

'You met a shower like I met!'

All I could do was burst out laughing!

'They made a mistake,' he said. 'You were doing fine. Well done.'

I never got any big criticism from the public. I never came face-to-face with anybody who had a serious go at me.

I always felt that I had a reasonable amount of support from the public. I might have got a few handy remarks but as regards hurtful criticism, I didn't hear any of it. I'm sure there were people that weren't happy but I didn't come across them.

It's something that happened.

It comes to a stage where you just say... 'Ah yeah'.

I don't engage with it.

It's long gone off my agenda.

I LOST INTEREST.

I wouldn't say I wished anyone bad luck but I just lost interest.

I went to the first game against Cork and they drew. The RTÉ camera picked me out straight away! I remember somebody saying after that Waterford got a goal and I wasn't cheering. I can tell you what I was doing.

As I always do, every time somebody gets a score, I was ticking it on the programme. It wasn't that I wasn't happy that we got a goal. Any match that I go to, where there's a programme, I tick off who did what.

That's the manager breaking out in me. Somebody pointed out to me that I wasn't jumping up and down. I don't jump up and down anyway. I didn't go to the replay.

I saw the Wexford game on television.

The next thing, I was involved with teams again. I would have gone to see Waterford when I could have gone to see them but I didn't have the same grá for it.

It wasn't bitterness, it was just that that chapter was over... let's do something else. I didn't let it eat me away because there's no point.

WATERFORD PEOPLE LIKE to win. I think they'd take anything now.

But if you can play with a bit of style and play well and produce a good product, I think they do like that. It probably cost us over the years.

The 2002 to '08 teams played great hurling but didn't win an All-Ireland. I believe the 1959 team played some fabulous hurling, should have won three and only won one. I felt that we were getting there as a team.

We were starting to put our stamp on it and then suddenly...

That was my style anyway. It probably comes from my football background; using the ball and working the ball. With the ladies football, we would have played that kind of a game. I would have watched other teams play and seen what worked for them. We knew we had to do something different.

We had to find a way.

Every manager will try to find a way that suits the resources he has. That's what we were trying to do.

If you don't play a decent brand of hurling, you're not going to win matches. I'd have my own ideas on that. The time has come that you have to use the ball well and you must play to your strengths. If the opposition have towering backs, you can't drop the ball in on top of them. You have to work the ball up the field.

People like Davy and Newtownshandrum started all that.

You play to your strengths. The day of the 50-50 ball is long gone. That should only turn up on the History Channel now!

Kilkenny beat everybody in the air for a good few years and then people decided we're not going to play Kilkenny in the air because if we do, we're going to get beaten. They had to find some other way.

On that night, we worked the ball very well, we used the ball very well, got good scores from out the field and put ourselves in a winning position. Unfortunately, we weren't able to finish it off. I really felt, leaving Thurles that evening, that we were in a very good place.

We were expecting to have Philip Mahony back. We knew Jamie Barron was going to be a serious player, and there was a couple more young fellas coming through like Austin Gleeson. We had a good minor team, they won the All-

Ireland later that year. They were starting to show what they were capable of.

I remember meeting Ned Quinn of Kilkenny four or five years before that in Croke Park at a football game… imagine meeting Ned Quinn at a football game! He said that Waterford have the best underage set-up in the country, it's only a matter of time.

So, I would have known there were good players coming through.

EVERY WATERFORD MANAGER has been unfairly criticised since Gerald McCarthy's time.

We have a lot of experts in Waterford.

Gerald got it, Justin got it, Davy got it, I got it… Derek got a lot of it, and Paraic Fanning got it. That's the way we are in Waterford.

All those websites and boards, Jesus, they would make you laugh. If you want a good laugh, have a look at them. They all want to do this, they all want to do that.

They remind me of pundits.

The analysis from *The Sunday Game* makes me smile at times. They make predictions before the game starts, change their mind at half-time and blame somebody else when the game is over.

And when do they have the answer?

At 29 minutes to 10 on a Sunday night, they have the answer. You know why? They've been watching it in a studio for the last five hours. A manager doesn't have that luxury, though.

The latest one is moving the players around the pitch on a screen. Imagine doing that in a game of hurling when there could be a deflection, a ricochet or a hook.

We're not playing a slow, boring game like soccer. As Justin said one time, soccer is a great sport. Turn on the television, it starts, watch it a few minutes, go out and cut the front lawn, come back in, 0-0… go out and cut the back lawn… come back in, 0-0… and you could have a big lawn!

In some of those games nothing happens.

The stakes are so high that managers are under so much pressure. That's why the game is getting so defensive. The coaching now has reached a level where, in a lot of cases, the teams are being coached to stop the other team playing, instead of coaching the team to win the match. The analysis has gone over the top.

I never let criticism bother me because I felt that some of the guys criticising didn't have a clue what they were talking about. I usually found that the good critics, you could talk to them and they'd make their point of view to you.

And there'd be merit in their point of view. The fellas shouting abuse?

Nah. I never really listened to it. Most of them are hurlers on the ditch or footballers on the ditch, so it never bothered me.

I never got any letters when I was Waterford hurling manager so I mustn't have been doing too bad!

I'm living in a remote area and there was no Eircode in those days!

PART FIVE

Cross Country

« CHAPTER 25 »

THERE'S A NEW challenge around every corner. There's always somebody looking for a manager or a coach.

A number of clubs contacted me.

Kilmallock in Limerick.

Bride Rovers in Cork.

Carrickshock in Kilkenny.

Piltown in Kilkenny.

I didn't fancy travelling… and the next thing I ended up driving to Westmeath!

I often did one-offs. I loved doing that. I went down to Ovens in Cork, to Éire Óg, Ciarán Sheehan's club and Daniel Goulding's club. I did a football session with them. We did a kicking drill and the kicking was very poor.

I said to the manager, 'How come nobody can kick the ball?'

'Sure, nobody kicks the ball now!'

'The teams that win kick the ball,' I said.

I went to Aghada.

I went to Youghal.

I went to Glanworth.

I was up in Wicklow. Willie Dilleen brought me to a number of clubs. He was a fella from Galway, who was working as a guard in Wicklow. He got my number and he rang me to know would I go up and take a camogie team for a session up in Wicklow. I went up a couple of times.

I was all over the place.

I went to Cyril Donnellan's club in Galway. Pádraig Pearses.

I went to a junior club in Galway city in Barna.

I went up to a Mayo club to take a ladies football session.

I went down to Gerald Griffins, a ladies football club in Limerick.

The Kilkenny ladies football team asked me down to do a session. It wasn't the highest standard but they were all genuine and they were all interested.

I did a good few sessions with Carrick Swans in Tipperary over the years.

I made great friends.

I WENT TO San Francisco on holidays in 2014; my daughter Sinéad was over there with her boyfriend, Ciarán Kenrick, now my son-in-law. The manager of the hurling club, Naomh Padraig asked me to take them for a session.

Ciarán was playing with them.

It was in a park across the bay in San Francisco. These fellas had no helmets on them. We did the first 10 minutes and it was terrible. I called them all in.

'Lads, this is shocking. Ye're all twiddling your thumbs… there's no one getting stuck in.'

The next thing, Ciarán got a lash on top of the head! There was a crowd of tourists passing and they were watching. After a while, fellas warmed up and they really got stuck into it.

'Gee' one of the tourists said, 'What kind of weapons are those guys using!'

'That's hurling, that's a sport,' I told them.

PADDY JOE RYAN, a great supporter of mine and a good friend, had asked me on several occasions to get involved with underage hurling and I didn't because I didn't have time due to my commitment to the Waterford ladies. Somebody asked me to get involved with the under-21 footballers in 2000, and I just said okay.

Declan O'Meara, Bimbo McGrath and Tom Cunningham came on board as well.

We did a little bit of training, we didn't do a tremendous amount of training but we had a decent group of players.

We were drawn against Kerry in the Munster semi-final in Dungarvan. We were three points up and time was up, and they got a late goal. That meant that we had to go to Killarney for the replay.

A week later. A Wednesday night.

I remember walking across the pitch… *We are going to win this game.*

Why, I don't know.

Gary Hurney was unbelievable on the night. He kicked a lineball over the bar. I'm led to believe that it was the first time ever that a Kerry underage team had lost a replay in Killarney. That was said at the time. But we won and we deserved it.

We got to the Munster final.

We played Limerick in Dungarvan. A huge crowd. Liam Kearns was in charge of Limerick. They had a lot more work done than we had. They had a couple of years of strength and conditioning done. We just never got going on the day. Seven points to four.

The following year we played Cork in Dungarvan. They beat us by four points.

After the game, one of our players swapped jerseys. Tony Davis was in charge of Cork. He came into our dressing-room after and he said, 'This is the most embarrassing day of my life, I'm going to have to ask one of your players for the jersey back… the Cork County Board are insisting that we can't swap jerseys'.

We duly found the guy, got the jersey and gave it back.

No money being wasted up in Cork in those days!

IN 2007, WATERFORD were Munster champions and they were entitled to a manager for the Railway Cup team.

Justin had no interest in it. I was asked and I jumped at it. They rotated the selectors in those days. I had Tony Hickey from Limerick and Alan Cunningham, who is Aaron Cunningham's father. We had a meeting in Limerick.

We said that we'd train for it, which wouldn't have been the norm in those days. Munster had moved away from that.

I rang a lot of players and the response was very positive. I had a good chat with Dónal Óg Cusack and he said he'd love to play but he was committed to something in England. I remember what he said to me.

'If Munster was good enough for Christy Ring… it should be good enough for anyone,' he said.

We contacted the players and we had a meeting in Limerick. I remember saying to the players, 'Not many people wanted this job, but I want this job!'

I suggested we train and everybody committed to it. We ended up training once a week in Dr Morris Park in Thurles for about six weeks. Everybody turned up. We got in Dave Moriarty, who was Limerick's strength and conditioning coach that year, and Alan Cunningham took the coaching.

If we were going to get involved, we were going to take it seriously.

Some of the Waterford players couldn't play; Ken couldn't play for instance because of the club championship. Brick played the first game and missed the final because he was with his club. Mullane was buzzing around the place and we made him captain.

Waterford had the captaincy anyway. We beat Leinster in the semi-final down in Fermoy and we played Connacht in the final at Croke Park.

Seán Óg Ó hAilpín rang me about 10 days before the match and he said he had a commitment opening a festival in Cork.

'We'll fly you up,' I suggested.

I contacted the Munster Council and they agreed to fly him up, but the plane was late. He only came into the dressing-room about 10 minutes before the match. We didn't start him but we brought him on very quickly as a blood sub and he played the rest of the game. He sent me on a lovely text after.

He said it was the only inter-provincial medal he ever won; thanked me very much, said it was a good set-up and he really enjoyed playing.

We had a good team. Lar was buzzing around the place. Mullane was flying. Maybe the few training sessions helped.

David Collins of Galway got a very nasty ankle injury. He was in savage pain on the sideline. Ger Loughnane, who was Connacht manager, got agitated and we had a few words, a bit of banter! It was full-blooded, no holds barred.

We went for it.

2-22 to 2-19.

They just gelled and there was a great buzz about it. The Munster Council put us up in the Croke Park Hotel and we stayed the night, and we had a few drinks. It was really enjoyable.

It was nice to work with elite athletes. These guys were amongst the top hurlers in the country at the time. We played Lar as a third midfielder in the second-half of the final. He got on a load of ball with his pace and he created havoc.

There was no messing; they treated it very seriously. Even talking to players on the opposition, they were mad to play it.

The Railway Cup was discarded too easily.

There was probably never a proper slot found for it. Maybe they should have left it in Croke Park on Paddy's Day. Anyway, it's dead in the water now. The GAA couldn't wait to get rid of it. There were 10,000 people at that game. That was the first game of hurling ever played under lights in Croke Park.

People might think that 10,000 isn't a lot but it isn't always about filling Croke Park. It's about the players, giving fellas the chance to play with fellas from other counties and representing your province.

It meant a lot to Mullane. He gave a very passionate speech after the match.

The following year Munster asked me to be a selector but Waterford nominated somebody else, I understand.

BACK IN 1984, I was driving along in the van one day with Séan Guiry and a fella called John Lonergan from Newcastle stopped me. He asked me would I be interested in doing a bit of coaching with Newcastle, our neighbours in South Tipperary.

It was my first time training a team outside of Waterford. I was just 28 years of age. A junior club, a small pick, fierce passion for the game.

We were playing a match one night in Newcastle, a league game.

Some fella hit one of the Newcastle players and he got sent off. He came out to the sideline and Minnie O'Neill met him with an umbrella down on top of the head! She laced him with the umbrella down on top of the head.

What can you say? A woman of 65 or 70 hit him with an umbrella!

He can't retaliate! I can still see the look on his face!

They had some support. Small club, massive support. I detected that there was more passion in Tipperary than there was in Waterford. It was like a religion in Tipperary.

One year, Newcastle had two very average players and they went for county minor football trials. I came back to Ballymac and there were three or four good young fellas sitting up on the wall and there were minor trials on in Waterford. I asked them how come they weren't gone to the minor trials.

They said they had no spin.

I said, 'I'll drive ye' but they wouldn't go.

There were three or four fellas who could have got on the team. The fellas from Newcastle didn't have any chance and yet they went.

I was there for a couple of years and I had great days picking teams with the likes of Mickey Nugent, Tommy Sweeney, Pat O'Dwyer and John Joe Nugent. We used to go into a barn in the village and pick the team.

We did our best and we won matches but we never had enough to win a county championship. We were beaten in the South final of the hurling in a replay by Carrick Swan's second team, and we were beaten in the county intermediate football final. Clonoulty Rossmore couldn't field so there was an emergency meeting in Newcastle called about whether or not to take the game.

'Lads… ye never won a county final, there's no point taking the game,' I said. 'We'll play the game.'

We got the game back to Clonmel, and we were beaten.

I was involved with the Moyle Rovers footballers for a while in 1993 and '94 with John Phelan and Bob Fitzgerald. They won the championship the year after. People used to say to me, 'They won it the year ye were gone'.

I used to say, 'Sure we had a good foundation put in!'

ST MARY'S RANG me up in December 2013, and off we went again.

Noel Buckley was the chairperson.

I went to school in Clonmel many, many years ago and I would have thought that they shouldn't be playing intermediate hurling with a base of probably 16,000 or 17,000 people. There had to be a decent hurling team in there.

I felt that if I could get a good coach with me, I'd take it on.

Somebody mentioned Tony Shelly's name. Tony played with Killenaule. The minute I met him, I remember thinking… *This man speaks the same language as me.* I knew he was a serious guy. He was a young, energetic, ambitious guy and I liked his philosophy on hurling.

It was a big challenge because hurling was very much the second sport in Clonmel. Football was number one. Commercials are very, very strong.

They knew that every year there was a chance of winning the senior football. You had a situation where you had two different clubs with the same players.

There was a bit of rivalry between the two clubs.

St Mary's would have felt that we should have taken on Commercials off the field but we wanted to make hurling training so good that the players would buy into it and commit to it rather than have conflict. We would have had a few battles with the management of Commercials over the years.

They were trying to look after their patch and we were trying to look after our patch.

St Mary's had been underachieving we felt. Billy Carroll was a selector, a really good guy, great fun and very well respected by all of the players.

Very soon, we realised that we would have to do something about underage as well. Tony managed the minor and I managed the intermediate. We had great times there. We won two county minor A titles, which had never been done before in Clonmel. It took us four years to win the intermediate championship.

Tony was a top, top guy. He had a great way with players but he was also very firm. When he said something, he meant it. He was full of energy, knew the game inside out, great to assess players and great to use game specific drills.

He'll climb the ladder to bigger and better jobs.

And we had a fella called Seamus Kennedy. Top guy, role model, really good player. He lived a couple of miles from where I lived out in the Nire Valley. His aunt is one of our best ever footballers, Áine Wall.

Seamus set standards on the pitch and off the pitch. It was great to have a fella like that around. In 2016, he got on the Tipp hurling panel after playing football for Tipp. He was so serious about hurling that he went to school in Thurles, which is a long way from the Nire Valley. That meant that his parents, Frances and Terence had to drive him to Clonmel or get him on a bus to Thurles or pick him up in Thurles.

They were that committed to him and to his career. He proved what a player can do if he wants to do it. He was an outstanding defender but we felt that we didn't have enough punch in attack so we moved him up to the forwards. He led the team. His attitude was, if you want to be a great player you can't do what some of your friends do. You have to be your own man.

Every time he trained, he set a very high standard.

We eventually took off in the fourth year and won a county championship against Gortnahoe/Glengoole. Tony had been coaching them a few years earlier so he knew the inside track.

We had a steady goalkeeper in Shane O'Neill, he was our captain. A good man to talk in the dressing-room. We had fellas like Jamie Peters, a really good lad. We had a lot of fellas that had experience of winning county finals in football and we tapped into that. The occasion wasn't going to bother these fellas.

Those two minor championships were very satisfying as well. The first one was against Kiladangan. The second one was in Semple Stadium against JK Brackens.

After one year in St Mary's, Westmeath came to me.

I WAS ON the go seven nights a week.

Three times with each, and sometimes four with Westmeath. I was driving every night of the week.

I would have tried to be at most St Mary's training sessions. Tony was more than capable of handling things but as a manager, you want to be there. The good thing about managing St Mary's and Westmeath was that you could decide what nights training was on! When you're the manager in both instances, you can avoid most of those clashes!

The following year we played senior B in Tipperary. We did okay but it was always going to take a while to adjust. There's a lot of good young fellas in that club who can have a great future if they decide to work hard at it. I had a great time in St Mary's.

We finished up in 2018 and then we went to Killenaule.

Tony is from Killenaule. We still talk at least once a week. I'd value his opinion. And he's a big Liverpool fan and I'm a little bit of a Liverpool fan!

We had a good panel of players but to be honest about it, we had a very poor year. The whole thing never got going. We lost the first match by two points and never got going. We won six or seven football games and football wasn't the priority up there.

We took the two teams. We had a good management team in place. My other selector was Declan Ryan, and Séan O'Regan did the physical training but it just didn't work out. I was disappointed with the way it turned out but that's life, that's what happens at times.

We played our first championship match against Kilruane.

We had three lads on the county hurling panel and three lads on the county football panel. On the week of the match, they were in twice with the Tipp hurlers and twice with the Tipp footballers.

So much for the GAA telling us April is a month for the clubs.

And then the story was they weren't training, they were in for meetings.

In the name of God.

The first time we really saw the whole panel was in the dressing-room before our first match. We met them in January and February, but from that until championship time, we didn't see them.

People can tell me that Tipp won the All-Ireland and that justifies it. Maybe it does but don't have Croke Park telling us ye'll have your players in April. In fairness to county managers, how can they release their players in April when they're playing championship the second Sunday of May?

I've seen both sides of it; county manager and club manager at the same time... St Mary's and Westmeath.

Those above in Croke Park are not in touch with reality.

They're living on a different planet.

« CHAPTER 26 »

I DIDN'T HAVE any intention of managing Westmeath.

Of all the jobs I was ever in, it was the most enjoyable.

After my first year in St Mary's, I got a call one day from Tom Hunt. He was the Waterford football goalie for a good few years and played for Munster. Tom was teaching in Westmeath and he asked me would I take a call from James Savage, the Westmeath secretary. He said they were looking for a manager and they were wondering if I would be interested.

My first reaction was... *Westmeath is on the other side of the planet!*

It's a long, long way away.

Out of courtesy, I agreed to take the call. James rang me up and asked could they meet me. 'Where will we meet?' I thought Portlaoise or somewhere.

'We'll go down to meet you,' he said.

These fellas are prepared to come down and meet me.

We eventually agreed to meet in the Horse & Jockey. I said that I would be courteous and polite. It was just so far away. It was the driving.

We had a meal, and a chat and swapped ideas. They suggested that I go up and see a few games. My mind was made up. I wasn't interested.

Outside the Horse & Jockey, we had another chat and I said to the chairman, Séan Sheridan, 'Lads, if I can do anything to help ye... let me know'.

'If you want to help Westmeath hurling, take this job,' Séan replied.

That struck a chord with me.

So, I went up a week later to see club games and I was surprised by the standard. The first thing that struck me was that they had a lovely stadium, a good crowd at the match, people passionate. And another thing was that these clubs had 35 players each togged out. Where I come from, you might be struggling to get 20 players on matchday.

They were all so enthusiastic. Some of them were good hurlers, more of them were only reasonable but the passion for it was there. I went home. James rang me once or twice. Then, I was asked to go up for an interview.

An interview?

I thought they wanted me to manage the team!

In fairness, they had to go through with it. I think it was in Tyrellspass Golf Club. I had a chat with them, told them what I thought needed to be done. On the way home, I got a phone call saying that the job was mine. I drove in the gate at home.

What have I done?

Then I broke the news to my family!

I got that phone call half-way down the road and then you have another hour to think about it.

This is five hours driving every night.

Part of you is saying… *How am I going to survive this?…* and the other half of you is excited by it.

These fellas are interested… let's see where we go.

I took it on for two years.

Then, I had to pick a management team. I knew nobody up there and I asked the board and the board said they'd get me selectors. I met various people.

I ended up getting a fella called Pat Clancy who was a really good hurler for Westmeath, who had experience of managing other teams, and Eddie Casey who was a livewire. He runs his own company that makes sportswear, EK Sportswear, and Eddie played football for Westmeath. The third selector was John Kennedy, another Westmeath player. Having met those three lads, I was happy with the management team we had.

I watched DVDs and looked anywhere I could to get information. Waterford played Westmeath in 2013 and for the first half hour, they gave us a good game.

I looked up their results and saw where they were. They were in a relegation play-off against Kildare to go down to Division 2B. I realised that there was a lot of work to be done. Next thing, I was driving up to meetings.

I needed a good coach. They told me that they had been speaking to Michael Walsh of Kilkenny, Ollie Walsh's son, who had managed under-21 teams. I met him down in Kilkenny.

I had met him before at the launch of DJ Carey's book. When I was Waterford manager, I was invited and he was sitting beside me.

The first time I met him I thought he was a very serious kind of guy. He was a quiet fella at first but when you got to know him, he's great craic and great fun. I liked his philosophy on the game. He'd been a good player, won a couple of All Stars, won a couple of All-Irelands and had seen the Kilkenny way of doing things.

He had been involved with Kilkenny underage and managed Carlow. Like myself, he had been involved with a Division 1 county and a Division 2 county. He said he would take it on. He had no reservations; he was very enthusiastic. He was a larger than life character, he would come bouncing out of the dressing-room, maybe do a little jig or a little dance!

He was a bit like myself, he wasn't completely wrapped up with all the fancy stuff and all the tactics. One of his great lines was… 'The most important ball you play is the intelligent ball'.

That might be 70 yards up in the sky, it might be 50 yards into space, it might be a 10 yard hand pass, but picking the best option was a big part of it.

The strength and conditioning coach was Peter Leahy, who would later became the Mayo ladies football manager. He was with us for the first year as well. Thomas Mount, a young fella in college, came in and did the stats. He was very good. We had a good set-up. Martina Seery came in as team secretary and did a good job.

WESTMEATH DIDN'T HAVE the resources that Waterford had.

If you wanted to play an internal game in Waterford and sent out an email to the clubs, you'd have 50 replies just like that.

That wouldn't happen in Westmeath because they don't have the players. You're talking about 10 or 11 clubs; eight of them at that stage were senior. The best intermediate team might be a club's second team. The best junior team might be their third team.

That's what you're up against. You had a small number of clubs, a limited pool of players.

There were things you take for granted in Waterford.

We had WIT for training with lights. In Westmeath, we had no access to a floodlit pitch with grass on it. We did a lot of our training on a 3G pitch in St Loman's, which was excellent, but it doesn't prepare you for a league game in the first week of February. It's a whole new ball game.

It was always a struggle to get grass pitches early in the year.

When the weather got better, we trained in Cusack Park which was perfect. We went to Abbotstown a few times and Athlone IT, but Athlone IT never seemed to be available and it was at the other end of the county for the players. We went to the Killucan football pitch and clubs would have done their best for us but there was a lack of training facilities with floodlights and that was a drawback.

We had our first team meeting.

We asked in 40 players and 38 of them turned up.

Straight away, these fellas wanted to do well. We started training in the middle of November 2014 and had a few challenges.

My first reaction was there's an awful lot of small men living around here!

Then I looked at the selectors and they were small guys as well! I soon realised that they were small men with big hearts.

Tommy Doyle was our full-back and he was about six foot four. From a very early stage, it was evident to me that these guys wanted to play for their county and they bought into it. They worked hard and they trained hard. The only thing was if somebody got injured or something happened, you were struggling for resources and struggling for replacements. Like every county team, but more so for a Division 2 team, you had four or five absolute key players.

Aonghus Clarke would have been on any team in the country. Tommy Doyle was a serious full-back. The Grevilles were good players. Fellas like Cormac Boyle would die for you. Liam Varley was an up and coming player and marked Maurice Shanahan the day we met up in 2013.

The first thing I noticed straight away was first touch.

The first touch wasn't as good, the fitness wasn't as good, the strength and conditioning wasn't as good. I always felt that it would take some time to do that.

We worked at that and you could see the improvement.

The way I approached Westmeath was first of all assess what you had and then try to build it up as you go along. Introduce different aspects and make it more professional.

If you go at full tilt at the very start, to get every aspect spot on, they won't have the commitment or the interest. You have to coax them and cajole them along.

In fairness to Westmeath, they did that. We introduced strength and conditioning and we upped that. Then, an extra night a week at training, nutrition and diet and all that. Bit by bit, we got there.

We implemented a gym programme.

I felt it was important that I went up a fourth night. I came up Monday night for the gym training as well. I was often in Mullingar four times in a week. In the worst of weather. If you're expecting players to do something for you, you must take the lead yourself. Michael Walsh would have been at practically every hurling session.

IT WAS JUST myself in the car.

Training was usually on at eight o'clock so I'd leave home at half four. It was two and a half hours of a spin.

If I left home at half four, I'd be there at seven.

I'd have something to eat in the Annebrook Hotel and be there at least half an hour before training started. If you started training at eight, you'd be finished about half nine.

Food, have a chat, leave for home at 11 and be home at half one.

Nine hours. I'd always be gone for eight or nine hours.

That was on a Monday for gym. There was Wednesday, Friday and I'd go up Saturday and stay Saturday night for Sunday. After a month, I didn't mind it.

I rang every one of my four kids on the way up. I had a hands-free in the car. I'd spend 15 minutes talking to each one of them; there's an hour gone... *Now I'm almost in Portlaoise.* A couple more guys I'd always find to ring.

On the way back, I might ring one or two of the selectors.

My golden rule was I wouldn't ring anybody after half 11.

And at half 11, I might be only in Portlaoise on the way back. Michael drove his own way because he was coming a slightly different route. I would call him on the road home too.

The first month, I wondered what was going to happen next.

It was new and it was different. The first challenge when you meet a new group of players is to learn their names. That takes a couple of weeks.

You have 35 fellas looking at you. Learn their names, get to know their habits and then get to know the players. Because if you don't get to know the players really well, you don't know what's happening inside their heads.

We started doing one-to-ones with the players.

We got a great response and they were very respectful. They were willing to listen, willing to learn and willing to work hard. Even though it was a struggle for the county board to keep two teams going, I always felt that they were serious about it as well.

There was serious club rivalry up there. Raharney, Clonkill and Castletown. That was never a problem. We did small things like mixing them up in the drills and even in the dressing-room, they couldn't sit beside a fella from their own club. Those things are important.

In our first game in the league we beat London, and then we went to Derry and got beaten. We stayed overnight.

That was a bit of a shock. Then we went to Kerry and we had to win. We won in Kerry and eventually we got to the final down in Limerick, against Kerry again, and we gave away five goals. You don't win finals conceding five goals. That was a big disappointment.

We had a penalty disallowed that day.

Brendan Murtagh took the penalty inside the 21.

I said to the linesman after, 'Jesus that ball wasn't inside' and the linesman said to me, 'T'was four inches inside it'.

Four inches!

Just when we'd worked ourselves back into the game. I felt like choking him!

OF ALL THE places I was ever in on this planet, an Appeal Room in Croke Park is something I wouldn't be recommending.

Niall O'Brien was suspended for the Wexford game in the Leinster Championship after an under-21 match, so we went to Croke Park to an appeal. As it was his last game at under-21 the rule said that he had to serve a two-week suspension which again is just ridiculous. How you could be suspended from playing senior after being sent off in under-21 just beats me. But nothing in the GAA ever surprises me.

It was my only time at an appeal in Croke Park.

James Savage went with me and Niall.

There was an atmosphere in that room that I didn't like.

We produced video evidence and, in my opinion, it never showed him striking. They interpreted it in a different way.

I remember saying to myself… *I'll never be here again because of the intimidating atmosphere.*

Funnily enough, we had another appeal later on and Michael Walsh went up.

He felt the very same thing.

He rang me on the way home and said, 'You were right'.

It was such an intimidating atmosphere that you felt that no matter what you said or did, it would make no difference.

The first thing I remember was, we had a video tape and they had no place to play it. Imagine being up in Croke Park with no screen! If I remember correctly we had to go to a different room and we saw it on a tiny screen.

In a stadium that holds 82,000 people, they hadn't a decent screen to show the incident. We ended up watching it on a mini screen.

I said to myself long before it ended that this was a waste of time.

Do they think they have to frighten people?

In my opinion, the onus in any of these things is to get to the truth. The GAA do an awful lot of things right but when they do something wrong, they are very slow to admit it. To turn the referee's decision around is almost like pulling down the moon. Back the referee. That's my interpretation, people won't agree but that's my interpretation.

I've always felt that when a referee gives a penalty or sends off somebody, nobody in the ground should be in any doubt. Those decisions have to be that clear cut. That's a clear sending off or that's a definite penalty.

Otherwise don't give it, otherwise don't send him off.

Our player was sent off for a trivial offence. It certainly wasn't deliberate and I would argue it wasn't even a strike. It was a mis-timed hurley without a strike.

We were missing four players against Wexford and Derek McNicholas was stretchered off in the second-half. That was year one done.

I was disappointed to lose the league final. That was the big one, that was the one we needed to win. I always felt that the first year was about trying to build a base.

« CHAPTER 27 »

I DIDN'T HAVE much luck with selectors!

The three lads stepped down. Eddie Casey had a young family with four children under 10 years of age and a company employing 35 people so he didn't have the time. Pat Clancy wanted to do his own thing. John Kennedy was a self-employed electrician who was sometimes on call. I lost the three of them!

Darren McCormack came in, another former Westmeath player. Adrian Moran was our other selector. I was a selector then on the under-21s with Adrian as manager. Keith Quinn and David Carr came in as kitmen and they were just brilliant. They brought such a level of professionalism. When you walked into the Westmeath dressing-room, your jersey was hanging up, your water and your programme were waiting for you; they took it to a new level.

Tommy Carr did the strength and conditioning, and he was excellent. He played football for Dublin, and managed Dublin, but lives in Mullingar. When I was told he was available, I went and met him. I called out to his house and had a chat. I always believe if you want somebody, go and meet them.

You have to make people realise that you're serious and that they think that they're good enough because you went to the trouble to go and see them. He managed Dublin, managed Roscommon, managed Cavan, played at a high level, knew what it took to get a team physically right. Our strength and conditioning improved and our mentality improved because he called a spade, a spade.

He was a really good speaker and knew what he was talking about. No excuses. He didn't do excuses or lame ducks or sad stories, or anything else. Be responsible for yourself.

We beat Carlow in the 2A final on a terrible day up in O'Connor Park. Ten points to eight. Brendan Murtagh got seven points. Terrible conditions.

That was a big win for us.

We won the 2A final but that year we had to play Laois in a promotion/relegation play-off. Win your division and then play somebody else. The system was changed after that. People will say if you're good enough, you'll do it but it isn't that simple. They had been playing against better teams all along so the speed of their hurling was ahead of us. It was on in O'Connor Park as well and they beat us 23 points to 16. We were 12-11 up at half-time but they took over in the second-half.

WE HAMMERED OFFALY.

Double scores.

2-22 to 1-11.

Fourteen points.

That sent shockwaves through Offaly. It was all over the national media for the following few days, radio and print. You'd think the world had fallen over.

The first thing I learned early on was that there was serious rivalry between Westmeath and Offaly. Offaly were the county that didn't have too much respect for Westmeath and they had the All-Irelands to show it. They had won four hurling All-Irelands but there's a lot more hurling clubs in Offaly than there is in Westmeath.

We were hopping in training. We played really, really well. We fancied our chances against anybody in Mullingar. We out-hurled them. It was one of those days when everything clicked. Eoin Price got 1-5.

He was one of Westmeath's best ever hurlers. He played shinty for Ireland. He was devastating that day. He could pick off points from out the field.

I remember being on the pitch after the under-21s beat Kilkenny as well. I thought the referee would never blow the final whistle!

They got a penalty and missed it. Andrew Gaffney got a last-minute penalty and shot wide. It was into the Dunnes Stores' end. I couldn't believe it when the ball went wide!

I remember saying to Michael Walsh, 'This is it!' Michael was wound up for it because he's a Kilkenny man. I remember thinking… *Jesus not again.*

Five of that Kilkenny team went on to play senior. Nine fellas played senior for Westmeath either that year or the year after. A high ball came in and a fella called 'Batchy' Warren Casserly poked it into the net.

We had a good core there. We played Liam Varley in the forwards for the seniors but he was outstanding at centre-back that night. There was some buzz.

That was another shockwave. Two shockwaves in the same year!

We lost to Limerick, 1-24 to 0-18 in the All-Ireland qualifiers.

When you get beaten by nine points, you can't say you could have won it but that wasn't a nine-point game. Brendan Murtagh missed a penalty at a vital stage. I always found against those teams that, in the last 10 minutes, they just had too much. Fitness levels, strength and conditioning counted in their favour.

We were back to four points with six minutes to go after missing a penalty. At the end of the day, the game is not played over 64 minutes.

We loved the opportunity and we always felt that we were able to stay in the game for so long, but we just couldn't sustain it. Usually against those teams, you're working so hard that eventually they wear you down. In the last five minutes, they always seemed to pile on the scores and that's what Division 1 teams do. Waterford played Westmeath in 2013 and we were level at half-time and ended up winning by 17. To sustain the effort takes an awful lot out of you.

In 2016, we played 15 matches, won nine and lost six. Three of those to top tier teams. In the Walsh Cup, we had half our players with the colleges. Imagine that? Imagine playing Galway and half our players with somebody else. That's what you call tying your hands behind your back. There's nothing you can do. You can moan and groan but you can't change the rules.

EARLY IN 2017, we lost Cormac Boyle.

He decided that he wanted to go with the footballers. He was an outstanding player for the first couple of years. He went to the footballers, did a bit with them but didn't get much game time. He came back to us but didn't have much hurling done and was nothing like the player he was the previous two years.

If a fella got a chance to play with the Westmeath footballers or the Westmeath hurlers, he would play with the footballers. There were a couple of footballers we asked to play hurling but they wouldn't commit. They wanted to play football.

We lost to Kildare above in Kildare. Joe Quaid was with Kildare. We had a bad day. It's a very unforgiving business. We won the next three games, including in Antrim, but we were out.

We qualified from the Leinster round robin on score difference. We beat Meath by two points on the last day. 1-18 to 0-19. That was a tough battle. The ancient historians told me that Meath and Westmeath were once part of the same Kingdom!

There was a big rivalry. Most of the Westmeath hurling scene is almost on the Meath border. Raharney, Castlepollard, Brownstown, Lough Lene Gaels, all those clubs.

I WAS SICK after the Offaly game.

We lost 4-15 to 1-20.

We gave away a terrible penalty. We all have days when things don't go well but we gave away a needless penalty; the ball was going wide.

Shane Dooley was on fire. 3-8. He was a really good hurler. If the opposition's leading scorer gets 3-8, you're not going to win the match.

When Killian Doyle got a goal to level it, I thought that we were going to go on and win the game. It was at a vital stage and we were coming from behind. It put us in a good position. We gave away a goal shortly after. Another mistake.

The goalie had the ball in his hand and was clearing it but Shane Dooley flicked it into the net.

It was hard to get over that. That was a low point. I was sick. A couple of desperate goals to give away.

On days like that, the journey home seems a lot longer.

It's like driving back from the moon.

Sick, sick… sick.

We left that one behind us.

We were drawn away to Tipperary in the qualifiers.

In the build-up to that game, we put a lot of emphasis on the performance. Semple Stadium was the place to play, where the GAA was founded. We went down on the bus.

I drove up to Mullingar to come back down to Thurles with the players. If we were playing in Carlow, I'd go up to Mullingar and travel on the bus with the players. I always think that's important.

The manager has to do that.

I remember our kit man, Keith couldn't park his van under the stand. He wasn't allowed to bring it in. He had to park it out on the road and carry in all the stuff. Keith and David were a bit annoyed about that because they felt it wouldn't have happened the other way around.

We knew we had to get a good start, and Killian Doyle and Niall O'Brien flashed over a couple of long range points early on. We played really, really well and then came that defining moment.

Cormac Boyle went through, and I think there was an option on the far side, but the goalie, Daragh Mooney made a good save.

We wouldn't have won the game but it would have been a much tighter finish. 2-18 to 0-15 is how it ended.

We played really well that night, got some good scores from out the pitch. That was a full-strength Tipp team. All you can ask for is to leave everything out on the pitch and that was one of the games that we gave it everything. We did all we could do.

Seamus Callanan was taken off right beside me and he didn't look a happy camper. Tommy Doyle had the game of his life that night. First to the ball, came out the field, took the ball out of defence.

People still ask me about Tommy Doyle!

'Where is that full-back ye had?'

A really, really nice guy. Maybe could have done with a bit more of a killer in him. He wasn't prepared to stick a fellas' nose in the ground. He didn't even realise how good he was himself. For a couple of years, he was in the top three or four full-backs in the country.

Aonghus Clarke and Robbie Greville popped a couple of points. Killian Doyle was a fantastic hurler. He had Division 1A wrists. The following year, he went to America for the summer.

In that Westmeath team, Paul Greville was the spiritual leader. He was a footballer, I had a chat with him and got him to play hurling. I reversed the trend with him. He had two more brothers on the team as well, Gary and Robbie. His first game back was against Kildare when things weren't going well.

He would have played for the Westmeath hurlers before and went on to play football. He was the Ken McGrath of that team. He was the fulcrum, a big, strong guy. When he spoke, people listened and he was a real man. A physical player who loved the physical challenge. Then you had Killian Doyle, Niall O'Brien, Aonghus Clarke, Tommy Doyle, a lot of good hurlers scattered around the pitch, and fellas like Cormac Boyle and Liam Varley, who would give you every ounce they had. Shane Power was corner-back that night. He has strong Waterford connections. His Dad is from Rathgormack. He was a hardy bit of stuff. The Powers from Rathgormack don't collect prisoners! Shane was in that mould.

A lot of good lads and their attitude was great. They just wanted to train and play for Westmeath. It was a big deal for them.

That's what I was looking for, fellas that really cared.

Fellas that got a lot of set-backs, lost big games, lost a league final and came bouncing back every time.

I HAD MY hip operation after that game. I'd been hobbling around all year!

Driving kills you. That year I had to stop the car three or four times going up to Mullingar and go for a walk because it was really sore and really painful. I was chewing Nurofen Plus!

When I'd get out of the car above then, I'd be in real trouble with it.

Thankfully, I went down to Tadhg O'Sullivan in Waterford, another great hurling man. The secretary used to say to anybody that went in with a hurling background that she'd cancel the next appointment because Tadhg loved talking about hurling! He did a great job and after 10 weeks out, I never looked back.

That was a tough year, because of the pain I had driving. I was hobbling around the place!

I didn't get anyone to drive me.

Nobody could listen to me for that amount of time!

I couldn't have all my chats on the phone!

« CHAPTER 28 »

ONE MORE YEAR. 2018.

This is it.

Alan Mangan came in as a selector, and was a revelation. A former county footballer in Páidí Ó Sé's time, he was full of energy and got on well with all of the players.

The most frustrating thing was we played a lot of good games but never quite finished it off. We lost a promotion/relegation play-off to Laois, lost a league final to Carlow and lost to Carlow again in Croke Park in the Joe McDonagh final.

We beat Laois in Portlaoise in the first round of the Joe McDonagh. It was the first time Westmeath had beaten Laois in the championship in 50 years. That was a big deal. And to beat them in *Portlaoise*!

It would have been nice to finish it off in Croke Park.

I'd been there with seven different teams. The Waterford ladies, the Dublin ladies, the Laois ladies, the Limerick ladies, Munster, the Waterford hurlers as Maor Foirne and Westmeath.

We were disappointed with that display; we were better than that. They won by five points but we never looked like winning that game. The biggest thing of all, for any management team, is to do yourself justice and we didn't.

Aonghus Clarke got a ball about a dozen yards out before half-time and blazed it over the bar. Nine times out of 10 he'd get a goal. Within 18 seconds, the ball was in the back of our net. At the start of the second-half, we gave away another goal.

For all the good defenders we had, we seemed to give away goals in big games. Ultimately, that came back to haunt us.

When the Joe McDonagh Cup came in, the coverage got worse. It was actually worse.

There's probably room on a Monday night for an hour's sports programme. If RTÉ can't cover it, let TG4 do it. Let them televise the games.

Coverage is so important. It makes players feel good about themselves and shows the product because there are some good games out there. If people don't know what the product is, they're not going to turn up to see it.

My last game was against Wexford in the All-Ireland qualifiers.

We played really well. I had bit of banter with Davy on the line as always!

We came back to three or four points and we were on a bit of a run. The thing about Cusack Park is hurling balls seem to go missing there a lot! Down over the apartments.

We came back to about three points and there was no hurling ball going in.

I shouted down to Davy.

'Throw in a ball!'

'We don't have a ball!'

'Ye had about 200 of them before the game started!'

He did a little war dance!

We gave them a decent game. At the end of the day, as I've said, the big teams will get you in the last five or six minutes. We always gave a decent game to the bigger teams but never really looked like beating any of them.

Limerick, Wexford, Galway and Tipperary. That's a different level.

I HAD MADE up my mind.

Four years.

Over 600 hundred trips up to Mullingar.

A total of 138,000 miles, which is from here to San Francisco 23 times!

That's a lot of driving.

I never looked at it like that, I enjoyed every bit of it.

It restored my love of the game. When you take in the travel, the time, the people I met, the attitude of the players, the way they wanted to be as good as they could be; the supporters, the clubs, the genuine people, it definitely does restore your faith. I was amazed by their passion for the game with such small numbers.

They love their hurling up there.

Above all the jobs I ever had, that was the most enjoyable. The Waterford ladies football job was enjoyable as well but it was more intense because we were in it at the highest level.

Fantastic times, great guys, good support from the county board. Billy Foley, James Savage, Séan Sheridan, everyone was so supportive.

I used to go into Jimmy Wallace's pub on a Saturday night. I wouldn't be a big drinker now. I'd be a three or four pints man. There would always be the same fraternity, a bit of a chat. They're very friendly.

A fantastic bunch of people, I couldn't speak highly enough of them. I always felt that if you treat people right, the chances are you'll get it back.

I still enjoy going back to Mullingar. I went up to see their first home league match against Waterford in 2020. I did the co-commentary for WLR and Shane O'Brien, the Westmeath manager, asked me to go in and say a few words to the team after, which was nice.

Earlier on in the year, he asked me could I go up and be in the stand with the stats man. My son was involved with Waterford so I wanted to give that a chance. I said when I could go up, I would go up.

I went up for the relegation play-off against Carlow. He invited me into the team meeting so we sat down and had a chat with the players, then I went up in the stand and we had a cup of tea and a chat after the game. They're very fortunate to have a fella like Shane and a top-class management team.

The disappointing thing for me was that the county team didn't have more support. We'd be talking about maybe 1,000 people at a Westmeath match. Whereas if you went to a Waterford challenge match, you'd have 3,000 people.

If all the spectators who supported the different clubs went to county hurling, we would have had a much bigger crowd. In 2018, there were more people at the Westmeath semi-finals than at the Waterford semi-finals. Big attendance. That was down to the club rivalry.

Having said that, when we played in Kerry or Antrim, Westmeath people got into their cars and a small number would have travelled to see those games.

There was some really good hurling men in Westmeath, like Billy Boyle. The clubs would always make their facilities available, but unfortunately a lot of them didn't have floodlights. They'd do anything they could for you. I always felt that I got fair press up there. If the team was poor, Gerry Buckley didn't spare us but he didn't insult us either. Very honest press.

In fairness to the Leinster Council, spearheaded by Nickey Brennan. They gave grants to counties like Westmeath but they didn't just throw money at it; you had to be accountable for the money you got.

It had to go into coaching, strength and conditioning, video analysis. I remember having to go to the Leinster offices in Portlaoise with the Westmeath officers and we had to present our plan. I'd like to see more resources being put into those counties but you have to be accountable for it, you can't just throw money at it for the sake of throwing money.

The other big thing around the country is there should be more coaching going on in schools. Hurling is a unique game. It's about first touch, it's about skill. You won't just become a hurler.

The Paudie Butlers of this world are priceless.

I would argue that when Peter Power was coaching in Waterford, he was the catalyst for that All-Ireland under-21 success in 1992 and what happened subsequently. I'd like to see five Peter Powers around Waterford now. Not fellas who have passed every exam on the planet and tick all the boxes. Peter went in and he didn't have 14 badges hanging off one ear.

He was a coach with enthusiasm, he got fellas out hurling and he encouraged the skills of the game. When he was in Ballymac school, there was a buzz around the place.

Coaching is key.

The skills of the game.

Fellas who are enthusiastic. I look around the country and I see all these fellas with all these badges and all these boxes ticked, but can they do a coaching session? In some cases, definitely not.

Paudie Butler goes around the country, he's a revelation.

Pat Moore in Waterford. A top class guy. Peter Power. We need thousands of those around the country. Can he train a team? Can he coach a team?

The other thing I liked about Westmeath was that the club championship didn't start until the county was finished. You might have to play twice a week but there's no championship matches in Westmeath until the county is finished. That means you're not starting off training in January to play in April, and not play again for four months.

You can start your pre-season in April and off you go then.

Why wouldn't that system work around the country?

You only have eight senior teams in Westmeath so you have until October to finish it. Instead, you don't have a big hullaballoo and all that nonsense about playing a match in April, one hurling and one football. No good to anybody.

What delighted the Westmeath clubs was, if a fella wasn't in the first 20, we'd release him for a league game on a Saturday. If we felt he might come on, we'd say go away and play half a game with your club.

The clubs were delighted with that.

We never stopped anyone playing club hurling because they were number 25 on the panel. Apparently, that hadn't happened before.

I WAS PRESENTED with a plaque as a parting gift by the players.

It was a classy gesture.

The inscription on the hurley was nice.

Thank you for all you have brought to our county. Your hard work, commitment and desire has shaped our character as men and instilled great belief within us. Four special years that will long be remembered. Westmeath hurling has been brought to a better place. We wish you all the best in the future and will always be forever grateful.

Usually when a manager is going out the door, they're firing hurleys after him!

It was lovely. It will always have pride of place.

I was honest with the players. I would have dropped a number of players off the panel and dropped some of them twice. I sent Darragh Clinton home twice and brought him back a third time. He was a young fella and needed to get his focus right, and he did.

I'd like to think that we found the right balance between being reasonably close to the players and keeping our distance. I never really went out socially with them. We had a few drinks at Christmas.

I was always at the end of the phone and kept in contact with them.

We had a good set-up and a good backroom team. The most important team that the manager has to pick is the backroom team. Michael Walsh was super; it was great to work with him. A very passionate guy. Eventually, we developed his sense of humour! He wouldn't be afraid to call a spade, a spade. He was very respected by the players as well.

The biggest thing of all was the players wanted to play for Westmeath. They had fierce pride in Westmeath hurling.

When you're working with people like that, it's relatively easy.

TWO MONTHS AFTER I stepped down, I got a phone call from Eoin Price and he asked me if I'd like to go on a team holiday.

'I'm not the Westmeath manager anymore and the Westmeath manager mightn't be happy with this.'

'It's nothing to do with him,' he said. 'We'd love if you came on holiday with us.'

I went to Tenerife with them! We had a great time.

Not many counties would ring you two months after you left to go on a team holiday!

Epilogue

I'D LOVE TO win one more All-Ireland before I die.

I didn't appreciate them at the time.

◄ ◄ ◆ ► ►

COVID-19 BROUGHT our family closer still.

We had a couple of Zoom quizzes. We'd all make out a set of questions.

Michelle and me had some battles!

It's okay I won!

If she got the better of me at draughts, she never got the better of me in a quiz! I'm happy enough about that!

When I used to be doing the questions at home for 'The Brain of Ballymac', I would hide them every night so none of my family could see them. The old favouritism thing again. I'd hide them so well I might struggle to find them two days later!

I missed the Sunday nights in the local and the few pints.

Everything stopped for a couple of months. I got a load of jobs done at home that I should have done over the last 25 years! I built a stone wall, got the back sorted out, tidied up the place.

We did a fair bit of walking as a family. All six of us.

Normally we wouldn't have time for it. Meet in the driveway and that was it.

It slowed down the whole world.

Everybody was gone mad. Running and racing around the place. Life was at a million miles an hour. Suddenly, people had to slow down.

It was a chance to catch your breath and reflect. What happens from now on remains to be seen but the world will never be the same again.

We had a little party for Louise and Iggy on the day they were supposed to get married. The wedding was postponed due to the virus... as Johnny Logan sings... *What's Another Year!*

◄◄◆►►

I DON'T KNOW will Croke Park ever again be full.

A lot of the older people won't go.

Even for All-Ireland finals, it will be a big test to see will they be able to fill Croke Park.

◄◄◆►►

I SAW A woman knitting one day in Croke Park.

At an All-Ireland final.

Offaly and Limerick.

Imagine that!

She took out a plastic bag, I thought she had sandwiches in it. She had no more interest in the match. Her husband was there beside her and he was interested.

Meanwhile, the person washing the jerseys and the person lining the pitch is watching in some pub because they can't get a ticket.

◄◄◆►►

I'D BE VERY surprised if there's any county manager making a fortune out of the GAA.

In county management, by and large, there's no problem.

My attitude was give me a couple of bob for diesel or petrol, even with county teams. This thing about a contract, I never had one. I got my mileage and something for a cup of tea but nothing major. I never wanted it.

Whatever other people are getting, they're well entitled to it. Every time anyone goes to training, it's a day's work. I don't know what they're getting, but they shouldn't be out of pocket.

People think that a manager's job is from the time you leave home until you get back home. But how many hours are involved besides that? A manager is responsible for 35 players, 20 in the backroom team, and has to chat with the county board, media and everything else that goes with it... and all the flak coming down the track at the same time.

There are stories of clubs paying outrageous money like €150 a session. That's ridiculous. You have the story then about every club should have a fella in his own club. Another ridiculous scenario.

If there is a good fella in your own club, the players are probably listening to him since they were 10 years of age. If he gets to 25, that's 15 years of the same fella in your ear.

They need a change.

Any fella who is in it for money, is in it for the wrong reason.

By and large, the vast majority of people are in it for the right reason.

There's always one or two but don't tarnish everybody with the same brush.

◄◄◆►►

ONE DAY I arrived unannounced at Brian Cody's doorstep!

'I have a favour to ask.'

'Come in,' he said.

He made a cup of tea, there were only the two of us. No sign of any trophies... typical Brian Cody.

I explained to him about the Shane Gleeson Awards in Ballymac, and he came up and presented them.

I did an interview with him on stage. It was like *The Late Late* with two armchairs.

I said to him, 'What was going through your head when Bubbles O'Dwyer was taking that late free for Tipperary in 2014?'

'I was wondering what he was doing taking a Kilkenny free!'

◄◄◆►►

I AM STRONGLY against ladies football joining up with the GAA.

Ladies football is exactly where it needs to be. I would be afraid that if they come under the one umbrella, they would lose their identity and the GAA would have too much of an influence.

The GAA could move it in a direction that won't benefit ladies football. It's so good, why do we need to change it?

Leave it there.

If in a parish, they all want to join up, great but treat every case individually.

I don't like to hear the phrase… 'the GAA family'.

'We're all part of the same family.'

The Mafia were all part of the same family as well!

I don't want to be too critical of the GAA because they give the LGFA the pitches and treat them very well. We've been very fortunate in Waterford. Since day one, the GAA has been very good to ladies football in the county. Successive chairpersons have been very good and we're never short of pitches, and we get the Fraher Field for county matches.

If a ladies footballer gets an opportunity to go to Australia, she should go. It's a once in a lifetime opportunity. It's a chance to play a professional sport and it's a chance to see the other side of the world.

Those things are a long way away from the Millfield where I started off in 1975.

I admire Cora Staunton, she's been a trailblazer. What she has done going to Australia has been incredible. She had a very bad leg injury and she came back again. And to do it at the age she did it? She's not exactly a new kid on the block anymore.

I would respect all she did in ladies football. She's really showed her true mettle going over there.

The players owe it to themselves to see what their true potential is and it's a fantastic opportunity to see a different culture. I'd be all for players doing that.

◄◄◆►►

I STILL HAVE a great grá for coaching, more so now than management.

I don't have the grá to drive around the country, miles and miles and miles again. I've driven for the last 40 years.

I love doing a bit of coaching and a bit of motivational stuff with clubs. I don't care what the grade is. If it's junior, I don't care. Once the people that are there, want to be there and are interested, that's the big one for me. I gave Colligan a hand a couple of years ago and they won a county junior football title. I got a great kick out of that, seeing other people happy and what it means to small clubs to win even a junior title.

When you go to one of the smaller clubs, who haven't won anything, and they get to a county final, you'd think the All-Ireland final is coming up.

The parish goat was even dressed up in the colours!

To me, winning a junior title is up there with winning a senior.

While I enjoy it, I'll keep at it. I know the time will come when I can't do it anymore. Health is the big one.

But there's still a buzz.

Getting up the morning of a match.

Getting your gear.

Getting your boots.

Sorting out the jerseys.

Heading for the match.

Being on time.

Making sure everybody else is on time.

I love the cut and thrust of a tight game when everything is on the line. There's a buzz in that. There's a great satisfaction in winning it and devastation in losing it; you'd feel like the world has just ended.

I often think of the last line in *Gone With The Wind*.

Tomorrow is another day.

◄◄◆▷►

I'D STOP IN a service station up the country.

Someone would look you up and down.

'I know you from somewhere.'

Crimewatch!

They'd want to talk about Mullane or Ken McGrath.

◄◄◆▷►

COACHING IS THE big one going forward for the GAA.

Get the coaching right.

Make sure the ball is involved in every part of that session. Because the game is played with the ball.

Lord have mercy on my old friends, Ned Power and Willie Prendergast, who started me on the road to coaching, the two of them are no longer with us.

I much prefer hurling to football. A lot of football coaching is about trying to stop the opposition rather than perfecting the things you should be doing yourself. Players don't kick the ball anymore and players don't kick points from 25 yards anymore. The good teams kick the ball.

Dublin and Kerry kick the ball.

If you want to win a match, you must be able to catch the ball, kick the ball and use the ball. Of course, play the hand passing game but there's so much more to it.

Above all, people forget that there's a set of posts at either end and if you don't put the ball between those posts often enough, you don't win the match. If you don't practice that, you won't succeed in doing it.

That's my theory.

◄◄◆►►

THERE HAS TO be a definitive club season.

The club has got to be on first.

It won't do to have the club second. Players will start training in October and stay with the county right through to August. What good are they to clubs then? They'll be flogged.

The ideal scenario is finish the club championship, run it from March to July, and then go and play county in August, September, October and November.

County finals over by July.

Croke Park is perfect every single day of the year. You can play there in December.

April was a club month.

That was a joke.

I'd put club first and get it done.

◄◄◆►►

CROKE PARK SHOULD have been opened much earlier and it should have been kept open.

There was €10 million to be picked up every year and to be put into development and coaching.

There would be no Lansdowne Road, that would be for pigeons! It wouldn't have been developed.

Some avid GAA people, even officers in this county, were ready to climb Mount Everest over soccer and rugby being played there. Instead of letting them in and charging the money.

That occasion when Ireland played England in the rugby, wasn't that fantastic?

In the 1970s, Thomas Crotty, Paddy Joe Ryan, Séan Guiry, myself and Willie went to at least one rugby international every season. It was a good day out. Something to do on a Saturday.

We went up to a match one day in Lansdowne Road and Ireland were doing badly. Moss Keane got the ball under his arm, tore up the field, flattened three or four of the opposition but eventually sheer weight of numbers brought him to ground, no support in the world.

The crowd went silent.

This Dub roars down

'Jaysus Christ… don't you know you're all allowed to join in!'

The banter at rugby matches was great.

One day against France, there was a French fella beside me and he took out a shot of whiskey, had a slug; next thing he passed it over to me and I had my slug!

I saw Barry McGuigan fighting for a world title, and I saw John Treacy win the world cross-country in Limerick.

Hire out Croke Park, charge them enough for it and put the money back into development at underage and coaching.

This is your fee, thank you very much.

Ten million euros every year.

It's a long time raising €10 million.

I'd be in favour of opening pitches across the country to other sports, provided it didn't interfere with GAA fixtures.

◄◄◆►►

WHEN THE COLLIGAN junior hurlers came to me at the start of the year, I said yes.

I had been giving them a hand, on and off, for a couple of years.

That stemmed from a friendship I had with people like Michael Wall, Paddy Ryan and Patsy Coffey.

It was great to be back on the field, and to work with a fella like Colin Dunford who was incredible. I've heard him get some criticism over the years, from Colligan people, not to mind people around the county. Alan Walsh did a great job as manager and we made Colin captain.

Boy did he respond. In every single game he was outstanding.

They're a nice bunch of lads. They're not the Kilkenny senior hurling team but they're a nice bunch of lads. Numbers are very tight. We got off to a bad start but then we went on a run and won the Western title... Colligan's first since 1985.

◄ ◄ ◆ ► ►

SOMETHING WAS MISSING.

It was tough to look outside Fraher Field and see people up on trailers, up on roofs of vans, up on a bucket of a JCB and putting up scaffolding!

I thought I was back in the building for a minute when I saw scaffolding!

I remember seeing a bit of scaffolding and the handrail wasn't great!

Those fellas went to that trouble to see matches.

◄ ◄ ◆ ► ►

I CAME BACK as Ballymac manager in 2020.

I was selector for two years with Michael O'Sullivan. I felt that this group of players deserved every opportunity to see how far they could go. Central to that was the management team I had with me; John Phelan, a great friend of mine from Grange, Mike Guiry and Caitriona Casey.

I had seen the players over the last two years and their attitude was very similar to what we had back in the glory days. They were every bit as enthusiastic, they were every bit as good to train. It reignited a spark in me again.

What keeps me going is a group of people who are interested, who want to work hard and who want to improve.

It's addictive really, it's in my blood.

Everybody knew the season was going to be shorter. There was no drudgery involved. They knew there was only a couple of months in it; the sun was shining, the weather was good and that made it easier for everybody.

We won our 39th county title in-a-row against Stradbally in September.

Stradbally beat Comeragh Rangers in the semi-final on merit, so we gave them full respect and we prepared well.

We spoke about getting an early goal to unsettle them, which we did.

It means an awful lot to our players and to our club.

We still get a great buzz out of it; we don't ever take anything for granted.

◄◄◆►►

I'D LIKE TO do a bit of travelling.

I was in Poland, and Berlin; I like those kind of places.

Four or five days just to see different cultures and different people. I'm big into history. That should be compulsory in schools because if you don't know where you came from, you probably won't know where you're going.

I wouldn't be interested in going to Australia. I was in LA, I was in San Fran… I was in Florida. Cities like Prague I wouldn't mind seeing for four or five days here and there.

Shane is very interested in the Super Bowl. I've been to a couple of soccer games and I couldn't face it. It's all so commercialised. I'd love to see a lot of those fellas on the dole! The money they're getting is outrageous.

Shane and myself went over to England on a trip. We went to Old Trafford on the Friday, on the stadium tour; went to Anfield on the Saturday, Liverpool and Arsenal, and went to Croke Park on the Sunday. Croke Park was miles ahead.

The soccer stadiums are cold, very little character and all the same. Croke Park is a work of art.

◄◄◆►►

THANKS BE TO God my family are healthy and happy.

That's a big one for me.

We've been going to matches watching our kids play for 25 years now and there's probably only a few more years left in that.

It's been magical. I still enjoy it just as much today.

If people get the same enjoyment out of coaching as I did, they'll be fine.

Many people have won more than I did as a player and manager, but I doubt anybody ever enjoyed it as much as I did.